Will's PIGEON SHOOTING

Secrets of consistent success

WILL GARFIT

Foreword by John Swift

Quiller

Copyright © 2012 Will Garfit

First published in the UK in 2012
by Quiller, an imprint of Quiller Publishing Ltd

British Library Cataloguing-in-Publication Data
A catalogue record for this book
is available from the British Library

ISBN 978 1 84689 123 6

The right of Will Garfit to be identified as the author of this work has been asserted in accordance with the Copyright, Design and Patent Act 1988.

The information in this book is true and complete to the best of our knowledge. All recommendations are made without any guarantee on the part of the Publisher, who also disclaims any liability incurred in connection with the use of this data or specific details.

All rights reserved. No part of this book may be reproduced or transmitted in any form or by any means, electronic or mechanical including photocopying, recording or by any information storage and retrieval system, without permission from the Publisher in writing.

Photographs by the author, except where otherwise credited. Artwork and diagrams by the author, except for Figures 1, 2 and 3, reproduced with the kind permission of Dr John Harradine.

Book design by Sharyn Troughton
Printed in China

Quiller
An imprint of Quiller Publishing Ltd
Wykey House, Wykey, Shrewsbury, SY4 1JA
Tel: 01939 261616 Fax: 01939 261606
E-mail: info@quillerbooks.com
Website: www.countrybooksdirect.com

CONTENTS

DEDICATION		4
FOREWORD		5
ACKNOWLEDGEMENTS		6
INTRODUCTION		8
CHAPTER 1	The pigeon family	15
CHAPTER 2	Background information	20
CHAPTER 3	Your gun and cartridges	34
CHAPTER 4	What kit do you need?	40
CHAPTER 5	Pigeon feeding habits through the year	63
CHAPTER 6	Pigeon shooting opportunities	83
CHAPTER 7	How to shoot pigeons	90
CHAPTER 8	A day out pigeon decoying together	95
CHAPTER 9	Flight line shooting	128
CHAPTER 10	An evening roost shooting together	130
CHAPTER 11	Favourite pigeon recipes	137
CHAPTER 12	Stories of memorable days	147
APPENDIX 1	Pigeon shooting and general licences	181
APPENDIX 2	Woodpigeon shooting – how does science help us do it better?	183
ASSOCIATIONS		186
FURTHER READING		187
WILL GARFIT PIGEON SHOOTING PRINTS		188
INDEX		190

Dedication

Dedicated to my wife, Gina, who whilst I spend many days out waiting for the sight of pigeons on the wing has, herself, grown wings of the angel of patience.

Also to the memories of, and gratitude to, my past friend and mentor the 'master', Archie Coats, who took me under his proverbial wing and helped me fly as I developed my passion, love and respect for the bird that provides such sport. He taught me to understand his mantra 'think like a pigeon', which is the secret to success.

FOREWORD

Shooting pigeons, despite their numbers, is no easy task. It requires careful reconnaissance, serious field craft and considerable shooting skill. Will Garfit possesses all these qualities in abundance. Here he has distilled a lifetime's experience into a magisterial guide to pigeon shooting that looks at every aspect of the bird, its behaviour and how to successfully tackle the vital task of controlling pigeon numbers.

Woodpigeons breed prolifically and move around the countryside rapidly in response to food availability and changing agricultural cropping practices. We see lots of them every day in both town and country. For many of us they provided our first experience of shooting, and our understanding of the countryside and the balance between man and Nature.

Pigeon shooting is essential for the prevention of serious damage to valuable crops. The range of techniques and their responsive and humane deployment are part of the equation, whether at the roost in winter or in the immediate vicinity of vulnerable crops - and all stations in between.

Pigeons can also be one of the most graceful birds. This paradox of woodpigeons as constituting a serious threat to crops, respected quarry of the sportsman and object of beauty for all, is one that has proved especially taxing for lawmakers, licensing authorities and pigeon shooters themselves. But this book is principally about how to do it, not the arcane convolutions of European jurisprudence and the general licences which provide for the shooting to take place.

I heartily recommend this book to anyone who shoots pigeons; for the experienced Shot it will open new avenues to success, for the novice it is essential reading.

John Swift
Chief Executive, BASC

ACKNOWLEDGEMENTS

First I would like to acknowledge and thank Andrew Johnston of Quiller Publishing and Jeffrey Olstead of the BASC for their vision for a new book on woodpigeon shooting and inviting me to write it in my way, not as a textbook but in a personal style, sharing my experiences over many years with my enthusiasm, passion and respect for the woodpigeon which produces such wonderful sport for many who shoot.

As this book was instigated by the BASC as a comprehensive guide to both experienced pigeon shooters and those wishing to learn the art of pigeon shooting, it is appropriate that John Swift, the BASC Chief Executive, should write the Foreword. I am grateful to him and he highlights the important role that the BASC plays in looking after the best interests of, not only pigeon shooters, but all who shoot live quarry whether for sport or crop protection.

A number of special people have helped to create this book with their own talent and expertise. Editing is an important part of producing a coherent text and in this case I am most grateful to Jeffrey Olstead for extensively tweaking the text to ensure that the instructional passages read clearly and that the whole represents the voice of the BASC. Also, thanks to Martin Diggle who edited on behalf of Quiller Publishing and Sharyn Troughton who has imaginatively and successfully designed the book.

I am most grateful to Dr John Harradine of the BASC for his two Appendices which cover the official line of the EU Annual General Licence, under which the woodpigeon can be shot throughout the year. Also for his authoritative comments of the science behind the selection of gun and cartridge to shoot woodpigeons most effectively and ethically.

ACKNOWLEDGEMENTS

Also, on authoritative science-based information, I must acknowledge the work done by Dr R.K. Murton and Ian Inglis and published in The New Naturalist series book *The Wood-pigeon* (Collins, 1965). Whilst significant agricultural developments have occurred since then, the biological facts relating to the bird have not changed and are therefore relevant to readers today.

Paul Stancliffe of the British Trust of Ornithology (BTO) has been personally interested in woodpigeon distribution and migration. His research and my observations have led us both to agree on this controversial subject.

Statistics from research published by the Game and Wildlife Conservation Trust (GWCT) have been important. I would like to thank Gillian Gooderham, who manages the National Gamebag Census, Nicholas Aebischer for his work published in the Journal of Applied Statistics in 1995 in which he 'investigates the effects of hunting on the survival of British pigeons and doves by analysing ringing recoveries' and Stephen Tapper who, with Brian Boag, published the report 'The History of some British Gamebirds and Mammals in relation to Agricultural Change'.

I am grateful to Dr John Harradine of the BASC for the information available in *Woodpigeons, Woodpigeon Shooting and Agriculture* (1997), based on his work with Nicola Reynolds, and also for his permission to use pie charts to illustrate points in Figures 1, 2 and 3.

Good photographs are an important element of a book such as this and I am most grateful for permission to use examples by three talented photographers, Charles Sainsbury-Plaice, Don Brunt and Rupert Watts. Other, less professional, photographs are my own.

I would like to thank my wife, Gina, for patience with my passion for pigeon shooting and for her selection of recipes. She is a wonderful cook and has included her favourites, some based on those from friends like Steve Wright, Tony Cooper, Andy and Kitty Hill. Others are those of Prue Coats, the doyen of game cookery, who has published several books on the subject and as the wife of Archie Coats was never short of pigeons on the menu.

Chapter 12 is a selection of articles from the *Shooting Gazette* for whom I have written a monthly page since 1995. I am grateful to the editor, Will Hetherington, for permission to use these as well as the sub-editor, Martin Puddifer who, for the last few years, has had to decipher my handwritten pages of A4 which drop on his desk by fax.

Finally, my grateful thanks to Veronica di Mambro who also has managed to read my handwriting and has typed the manuscript to evolve on screen in a way that has allowed those involved at Quiller Publishing to have created this book.

INTRODUCTION

Starting from the premise that the woodpigeon is the prime avian agricultural pest and does serious damage to crops throughout the year, it is not surprising that attitudes to the bird fall into two camps. Most farmers hate the woodpigeon, yet there are many of us who find it the most fascinating and sporting bird in the world; not only because it can produce every variety of shot in the book but because the shooting is only one part of the challenge. For you, the pigeon shooter, to get into the right part of the right field, on the right day and at the right time of day creates so many elements of decision based on reconnaissance, fieldcraft and experience. It is therefore a sport you make for yourself. So satisfying if one gets it right, culminating in good shooting despite the many factors that can undermine the perfect day against this clever bird. I hope that in this book I can help to address the many varying factors that can make or break a day whilst sharing my love, enthusiasm and respect for the bird itself. I am not a professional pigeon shot but an enthusiastic amateur. Over the years I have learned what works for me to shoot consistently good average bags and hope to pass on these ideas to you.

My passion for and interest in the woodpigeon started at an early age and my earliest memories were of when, aged about 10, I was fascinated to watch as a group fed on the robinia flowers late on June evenings outside my bedroom window when I was supposed to be asleep. Each bird would ponderously but carefully sidestep along a branch and either stretch up or twist down to reach the hanging racemes of white flowers.

However, the next experience awoke the heart of the hunter in me as, when walking in the woods, I met a man standing silently with a gun, hiding in the thorn bushes near a prominent ash tree on the woodland edge. There were half a dozen dead pigeons at his feet and I could see an old wooden

INTRODUCTION

decoy out on the grass field. He was a typical countryman of the past who went out occasionally to pot a few pigeons for a pie. Cartridges were saved for shots at birds sitting in a tree and this dear old man was pleased with the morning's bag. I, too, could see the excitement of fooling a wild bird to come as you waited to get a shot and hopefully have a few birds with which to arrive home triumphant.

The next big step coincided with me reading avidly any pigeon shooting articles in the *Farmers Weekly* magazine which I shared with a school friend, a farmer's son from Yorkshire. There were black and white photographs of a man in a pigeon hide in Hampshire and stories of him shooting bags of pigeons I had never dreamed of. This man, Major Archie Coats, was to become my hero and later my guru and friend – but more of him later.

One afternoon, while playing cricket at school on a ground surrounded by fields and woods, I heard the odd shot or double shot being fired from a group of trees in a hedgerow a few hundred yards away. Not being a bowler, afternoons spent fielding seemed rather monotonous to a teenage boy wanting more action than the occasional run to the boundary or walk across the pitch at the change of an over. So, at the end of the game, I crept along the hedge to where I had heard the shots. I came up behind a man peering out of his hide watching for the occasional pigeon to fly past and swoop down to his decoys set up on a patch of laid wheat. He was very patient, not only for a shot but with me endlessly asking questions. Every now and then a bird would come into view below the canopy of the overhanging trees which hid and shaded us. It swung round to approach the decoys and he would take a shot – usually successfully adding the bird to the bag and leaving a puff of silver feathers hanging in the air. Though I had never fired a shotgun I was hooked.

Despite a late start in shooting compared with some people, I had always harboured a fanatical enthusiasm for any form of human skill with a projectile. When 6 or 7, I spent hours alone on a beach each summer learning to throw stones accurately. Later I honed my skills with a home-made bow and arrow or catapult and even throwing knives. All had the advantage of being silent and all led to the demise of some creature with fur or feather. I am, not, of course, suggesting this as a way in today's world of learning the art of fieldcraft or hunting skills. In those days activities like collecting birds' eggs were encouraged for boys growing up in the countryside as being healthy pursuits which led to an interest in Nature. We were not at risk of contravening any EU law and learned to use discretion and create our own codes of practice to ensure that species did not just survive, but thrived. So I do not apologise for what now is illegal but then encouraged many of our

leading conservationists of my generation, whose understanding of the natural world was learned on the ground and did not need a university degree to see the proverbial wood from the trees.

When I was 12 or 13, my father taught me to shoot safely with an air rifle, a .22 BSA Cadet. This, with open sights, meant I could control sparrows or rats in the next-door farmyard, as well as the odd unlucky woodpigeon. When I was 17 father borrowed a single-barrelled .410 which lit the blue touch paper of my shooting career. I learned to stalk pigeons sitting in trees, along a hedgerow, or coming to roost in a little wood. In winter it was easy for them to see me and in summer the leaf cover made it difficult for me to see them. However I learned many important lessons of fieldcraft and a lifelong respect for this wily bird. The thrill developed as I acquired the skill to shoot flying birds with the little .410, but cartridges were expensive so I was a quick learner as I could not afford to miss too often.

One evening I waited with my father for pigeons to flight over the corner of our orchard on their way home to big woods some miles away. I had heard of the lead one needs to give a high-flying bird and felt I had overdone it as I swung the gun what appeared to be eight or ten feet in front and fired. A little pop and for a moment the world stood still before the bird lurched in the sky and planed down, to be retrieved away back in the meadow behind the church. I still carry that mental picture of the lead I gave that bird and the surprise that it worked – but it has worked on many high pigeons since, with any calibre of shotgun.

Today, youngsters and those taking up shooting can easily visit their local shooting school where trained instructors can arrange for any pigeon of the clay variety to simulate every target to be encountered in the field. This is definitely the way to learn to shoot, but did not seem to be an option when I was young. So I taught myself via the chain of boyhood skills described through air rifle, .410 and finally 12 bore.

Soon after I was married, in my early twenties, my father-in-law felt he would like to experience the sport of my passions. He booked a lesson at the West London Shooting School and invited me to come along. I had never seen or fired at a clay, but what a revelation. Our instructor was the legendary Percy Stanbury. I did not know of him then but he had won virtually every clay competition in every discipline in his day. When instructing he never fired a shot, but his demonstration of gun handling, footwork and balance transformed shooting from an action to an art as I watched. Like a ballet dancer he would pirouette from side to side as he moved so lightly on his feet and the gun itself was just an extension of the swing that emanated from the ground through knees, hips, shoulders to the tip of his barrel – a lesson for life.

INTRODUCTION

At this time I heard from one of the instructors at the West London Shooting School that Archie Coats took people out for a day for a fee. This was the excuse I was looking for to make contact with the great man and, after some difficulty finding his address, I wrote to him telling of my enthusiasm as a young but fairly inexperienced pigeon shot. I received a reply scrawled on a postcard in near illegible writing. However I eventually deciphered the content, which kindly suggested I come on a certain day in June and, in true military fashion, he gave me a six-figure map reference of the house and instructions that I should be there for breakfast at 0800 hours. In excited anticipation I did not sleep much the night before but was punctual and both Archie and his wife, Prue, welcomed me warmly and after one of Prue's great breakfasts we set off for a day on a field of seed grass on the nearby estate.

Archie Coats in Action

It was a square field with woods on two sides and Archie set me up in a hide under the trees on the western edge with fifteen dead birds as decoys. Pigeons soon appeared and some decoyed well. After an hour or so Archie's Land Rover drew into the gateway opposite, having been on a reconnaissance of other fields nearby. He watched me shoot a few birds before driving over to ask if all was well. He had been pleased to see me kill the birds he had watched but asked why I had not shot at the birds passing over me along the tree line. I said that I had not seen them to which he replied, rather critically, that I should keep my eyes open. He then went and set up under the trees on the other side of the field at right angles to my left. He shot virtually everything that came, except he did not seem to shoot at the birds flying overhead. After two hours he came over and suggested that as I was still not shooting at the birds over my head we should swap places. Obviously they were out of sight above the leaf canopy and I could not be cheeky enough to suggest that he, too, had failed to shoot at the equivalent birds passing over him.

The day continued with us each having an even amount of sport. Still neither of us took the birds above us but eventually he accepted that neither of us could see these birds to shoot them. Nevertheless, we picked about ninety pigeons from each hide and then came the moment at the end of what had been my best day ever, to ask how much I owed. As an impecunious art student at the time I realised I should have enquired earlier. The Major, as he was known to most, just smiled and told me to help myself to his cartridges to refill my bag and said it was good to have someone who could shoot straight. He would not accept any payment and said he hoped I would come and help again. So began our great friendship and I often skived off from art school for a day to join him. He and Prue became like second parents and I loved them dearly. Visits to Towerhill in Dummer near Basingstoke were very special and I learned so much about the job of pigeon decoying and to 'think like a pigeon' – his great mantra. There were good days and bad, known as 'Major disasters', but all were enjoyable and had a lesson for me, his disciple. I was slow to understand from school the greatest lesson of all, which is that education is only the beginning and preparation for life, to 'learn to learn' – so, forty years later, every day in the field has some little lesson to build on those wonderful early experiences with Archie Coats.

Whilst not wanting to bore you with my early experiences of the countryside, the woodpigeon and shooting, the fact is that I have developed an immense respect for my quarry, whatever bird or animal that may be. Throughout history this is a key element and a common factor of all the greatest shots and hunters, from the Stone Age hunter gatherers who

INTRODUCTION

Good advice from Archie Coats 'learn to ...'

celebrated their quarry in cave paintings, to African tribesmen, Aborigines, elephant hunters, the most skilled fishermen, rabbit or mole catchers. Every creature captured, whether for food, sport or control, has its own story. To me the woodpigeon is the ultimate species I have experienced to challenge the hunter by its sharpness of vision, speed of reaction, variety of flight, life history and subtle beauty. This is my book to celebrate such a special bird and the sport it can produce. Though the pigeon is such a problem to agriculture we can definitely help the farmer and derive great pleasure and satisfaction in doing so.

I now want to introduce the concept of 'you'. I am writing this text as if in a letter, not to all but to the individual 'you'. We will be going pigeon shooting together in some chapters. We will be discussing the merits or otherwise of various items of kit and equipment. However, I have no role in selling anything to anyone, except the concept that maybe my enthusiasm and lifelong experience could help you in whatever capacity you shoot and importantly, learn to learn, as every day has a new lesson while trying to outwit the wily woodpigeon.

The inspiration for this book came from Jeffrey Olstead who, on behalf of the BASC, invited me to write a small instructional book for people interested in taking up the sport. In principle that seemed a good idea, but it sounded rather formal and like a guide or textbook. That did not suit my more

personal and informal style of writing, which made me hesitate in immediately accepting the challenge. The other fact was that I felt the pigeon such an exciting, interesting and sporting bird that maybe my wider thoughts and experiences over the past fifty years could be more helpful if produced in line with my two previous books, *Will's Shoot* (1993) which became *Will's Shoot Revisited* (2005) and *Will's Shooting Ways* (2009). Andrew Johnston of Quiller Press, who published the last two of these, was very positive in his support and agreement as indeed was Jeffrey Olstead. I hope therefore that this book will be both instructional and an interesting read for all, whether BASC members or not (although, if not, then I strongly recommend joining). The result will, I hope, bring you great satisfaction and sport, as well as providing relief to the farmer over whose land you are successfully protecting crops. So here's wishing you good shooting and safe shooting.

Man and boy – the enthusiastic team with a lot of good pigeon shooting memories to share. (Rupert Watts)

CHAPTER 1

THE PIGEON FAMILY

The woodpigeon (*Columba palumbus*)

So let us look in detail at the woodpigeon in the hand. We all know how to identify it but it is more than a mid-sized grey bird with white neck ring and wing bars. It is 15in long with a wingspan of 26in. The wings are long enough to create speed when necessary but broad enough to enable agility in the air in combination with its tail length, which can fan broadly as an airbrake yet is streamlined in general flight. It has a broad chest for its size to carry large pectoral muscles either side of its deep breastbone, so it is a strong-flying bird. These basic anatomical details explain why it can fly a long distance with ease and can use the wind to fly at great speed under control. This is important for survival when threatened by avian predators such as the peregrine or sparrowhawk, though inevitably some succumb. Its agility enables easy flight within woodland which, after all, gives the bird its name. For us pigeon shooters it therefore has the ability to produce every shot in the book as a challenging and sporting quarry.

You do not need to be an artist to appreciate the beauty of the bird from head to tail; its subtleties are there to be enjoyed by all. The head is comparatively small for a bird of its size, a mid blue-grey all over, with bright yellow eyes with small elliptical, not round, black pupils. The beak is of medium length, pinky mauve at the tip, giving way to yellow-orange and with white fleshy lumps at the base, which cover the nostrils. The bill is functional, with a down-curved sharp tip to the upper mandible and converse curved tip of the lower. A perfect tool for feeding on a large range of natural food it can pick up easily or extract from pod or ear, or with equal ease pick or tear vegetation into bite-size pieces. Just look at the variety of food in a pigeon's

crop over the year and it is obvious that it not only survives but gastronomically thrives in all but the harshest winter conditions. But more of seasonal food later.

The neck is perhaps of average length for a bird of this size but with an obvious crescent of white feathers either side, which show up at a great distance not just to man but to fellow flock mates. This white neck ring sends spontaneous messages. A steady bobbing of the head of feeding pigeons encourages others to join the party. But if the birds become suspicious they immediately lift their heads, exaggerating the neck band, and hold them still as a warning. This is easily interpreted by others as a sign to be wary but not necessarily alarmed. The neck band is probably also important in the courtship display when the male bobs and bows his head, an action which will alternately reduce and expand the visible white ring.

Coo-cooo-coo, coo-coo

On the upper side of the white neck band is a beautiful iridescent viridian green, while below, in sunlight, there is the shimmer of pinky-purple. The back of the upper body is of darker mid-grey (which, in young birds, is more of a brown). The same grey extends to the secondary feathers where, across the mid wing, is what ornithologists call a transverse white band. Outside that are long dark, grey-to-black primary feathers. The white wing bars are definitely the visual alarm signal as, with fast wingbeats, the bird makes a rapid retreat. Equally, when approaching a flock of feeding birds, the slower wingbeats or gliding flight shows the wing bars, indicating to others following that all is well to land and join in the feast.

The rump of the bird is a light silvery blue-grey, contrasting with the darker grey above. This then fades as it becomes part of the outer tail feathers, which have a similarly light inner grey ring when fanned.

The breast and underpart of the woodpigeon is beautifully subtle as the upper breast to the neck ring is grey-purple that merges to become a lighter plumage of a soft pink coral mauve. This, like a soft watercolour wash, gives

THE PIGEON FAMILY

way to light silver-grey feathers which extend down under the tail. Short, strong, pink-purple legs and feet with black toe nails are distinctive. The underwing is a light blue-grey that matches the rump.

In all, the woodpigeon is a bird of great beauty, from the most subtle colours of the breast plumage to the strong, almost heraldic black, white and silver of the upper wings and body. Beautiful too is the black and gold eye set in its proud but avaricious head. If this were a rare bird it would be described and acknowledged as a very beautiful species. Another interesting observation is that, when seen at close range, feeding on a lawn or in a park, the grey head and back of the bird seem to light up with a form of bloom as of the finest of velvet.

As an artist I perhaps paint a prettier picture in my description of the woodpigeon than would my farmer friends, who just use one word 'blue' with pigeons on a field. However, that description is enough to get us pigeon shooters excited!

So, can we confuse the woodpigeon with any other bird in the field? With experience, no, but there are six other species of pigeon you may encounter. However, while some are similar amongst themselves, they differ considerably from the 'woody'.

The stock dove (*Columba oenas*)

The stock dove is a charming little dove, smaller than the woodpigeon. It is basically dark grey all over except for darker wing tips and the end of its tail. Close up it has a brilliant iridescent green neck. However, the key identifying features are the smaller size than the woodpigeon and the lack of white wing or neck markings. It used to be shot but this changed in 1981 when the Wildlife and Countryside Act gave it protection. Prior to that, the 'stocky' or 'blue-rock' as it was often known, was a frequent visitor to the same fields as woodpigeons. They were never shot in the same numbers as the woody and actually did little damage to farmers' crops. Their numbers stay buoyant and they are common in woodland, where they nest in holes. They make a distinctive if rather monotonous cooing – 'Ooo-ooo' – with the timing of a purring cat. So when out decoying pigeons, look out for this smaller slate-grey bird with no white wing bar or neck ring. The stock dove may arrive singly or in pairs, rarely in groups and never in flocks, but this dainty flying bird will come to your woodpigeon decoys and is the species most easily misidentified as it arrives and hovers over your pattern – but do not shoot this protected bird.

The feral pigeon *(Columba livia)*

This bird is a descendant of the true rock pigeon and its Latin name is the same. It was probably originally domesticated as the bird of medieval dovecotes, where it was managed to produce tasty meat. From that domesticated state it was a short step to it becoming a common town bird to the point of being a tourist attraction in Trafalgar Square. There, little bags of corn were sold for people to hand-feed these birds of many mongrel colours. More recently, as numbers increased in inner cities, it has been perceived as a disease-carrying pest rather than a tourist attraction. Ferals can vary from dark to light grey with white patches anywhere on their bodies.

This bird is not protected and, as with the woodpigeon, can be shot with permission of the landowner or farmer under the terms of general licences (see Appendix 1), and farmers with fields adjacent to towns are often keen to see them controlled as they eat seed crops. However, in such a situation be careful not to shoot a stock dove by mistake, as these can look very similar to a grey feral.

Racing pigeon and ornamentals

It is important when out shooting not to shoot racing pigeons, which will be seen flying fast in tight groups. These are birds with a purpose, to get home as fast as their wings will carry them as they navigate with amazing accuracy over many miles to their home lofts.

We should also avoid shooting birds that arrive in a group and include pure white and other selected colours – they are probably from someone's garden dovecote. These ornamental doves are more difficult to identify and, while they can be classed as feral if not around their home, it is diplomatic not to shoot them.

The rock pigeon *(Columba livia)*

This protected species is rarely found except around the coast of Scotland or the outer isles and in these locations there are very few woodpigeons, so misidentification is not an issue.

The rock pigeon is the same size as its descendent, the feral, with which it shares the same Latin name. However, it is paler grey on the back and upper

THE PIGEON FAMILY

wings, which have two conspicuous black wing bars. The rock pigeon has pale under-wings and a white rump. It is interesting to observe a group of ferals in a town park and see how many have the original coloration characteristics of their forebear, the rock pigeon. In years gone by some sportsmen enjoyed shooting them from a boat as they were disturbed from their coastal caves. This would have been very challenging, as to shoot a bird which could fly very fast, while the Gun was bobbing about in a small boat on the ocean, would require considerable skill. However it is a charming bird and not common except in the rocky coastal habitat, so it was worthy of protection.

The turtle dove *(Streptopelia turtur)*

The fifth species that could be seen is the turtle dove. This small, slim, brown dove used to be common in the agricultural landscape of Britain but is becoming increasingly rare. I always feel its distinctive 'churring' is a real sign that summer has arrived, as it is not heard until May. The turtle dove migrates north from wintering south of the Sahara in Africa. It is a charming little bird with a flittering flight and appears to be slim, with pointed wings and tail. This bird is definitely protected and a sighting is to be cherished as its population has crashed in recent years.

The collared dove *(Streptopelia decaocto)*

The sixth species is the collared dove. This bird was never around in my youth, but colonised Britain in a remarkably short period in the 1970s and 80s and is now found from Lands End literally to John O'Groats. It is a light buff-brown dove with distinctive black neck ring and wing tips. In shape like a turtle dove, it is larger and easily identified by its size and lightness of colour. It can legally be shot and, although it is more common around farmyards, it does venture out into open fields. Since farmers have had to protect corn effectively in their barns from pests the population of these opportunistic birds has declined.

So, to summarise, those species that can be shot are the woodpigeon, feral and collared dove. Those definitely protected are the stock dove, rock pigeon and turtle dove. Those to be avoided are the racing pigeon and tame garden dovecote pigeon. Like any good wildfowler, ensure you know your quarry species.

CHAPTER 2
BACKGROUND INFORMATION

What's in a name?

The woodpigeon is also known as a 'ringdove', in Scotland as the 'cushat', 'cushy-doo' or just 'doo', whilst in Wales it is the 'quist' or 'queest'. For many it is just affectionately called a 'woodie'.

Interestingly, different authors have written the bird's name in a variety of ways. Dr Murton, in his authoritative New Naturalist book *The Wood-pigeon*, hyphenates the two words, as does the Oxford dictionary. Colin Willock, in his 1995 work *The Book of the Wood Pigeon* (which I illustrated), split the name into two separate words. Ornithologically, the comprehensive *Collins Bird Guide* spells it as one word 'woodpigeon'.

Pedantic it may be, but fascinating as, over the years, a number of books on pigeon shooting have been published. I have collected every one and they have chosen to refer to *Columba palumbus* as follows:

Wood-pigeon	Oxford dictionary, Murton, Brander, Arnold and Johnson
Wood Pigeon	Willock and Coats
Woodpigeon	Collins, Theobald, Baker, Batley, Coles, Humphreys, Gray and Hall

So there are eminent authorities in each of the three camps. I respect everyone's view but personally will go with the majority, i.e. 'woodpigeon' as one word. At least all agree with the Latin name *Columba palumbus* and for most of us the 'woodie' will do. Also, in this book, when the reference is just to a 'pigeon', you can assume it is the bird of the woods, the woodpigeon.

BACKGROUND INFORMATION

History

The woodpigeon is now the most serious avian agricultural pest, but was it always a threat to crops? The answer is probably not before the eighteenth century. However, let us step back in time to find references to the woodpigeon. Certainly the dove, in different forms, has been an important bird for food and sacrifice. Egyptian tombs depict doves and the Bible has many references to them, the most obvious being the lovely story of the bird returning to Noah on his ark carrying an olive branch in its bill. This, we know, signified that the bird had found land within flying distance and thus has became a symbol of hope, now extended to the hope of peace in conflicts throughout the world. However, to me, the interesting question is why was it carrying an olive branch? The answer is that it was bringing it back as nesting material and that the land found would produce food for rearing a brood. That instinctive act by the bird certainly indicated hope for its species as well as kindling Noah's optimism for the future of Mankind and all his animals.

For thousands of years it is likely that doves in one form or another have been an important food source whether hunted, caught in traps or kept in forms of dovecote.

The woodpigeon as a species would have existed for many thousands of years, ebbing and flowing north or south depending on Ice Ages. So the bird we know today would not have colonised Britain until after the last Ice Age 10,000 years ago and would have followed the trees as the original forest moved north. Those birds would have been true 'wood' pigeon, not only roosting and nesting in trees but surviving almost entirely on woodland food. There would be leaf buds in spring and summer, fruit and nuts in autumn and through to the winter, when ivy berries would become an important addition to the winter and spring diet as they are today.

Obviously pigeons could not feed on crops until man evolved from hunter gatherers to agriculturalists who cleared areas of forest in order to grow crops. The woodpigeon population would have been low, similar I suspect to areas of Britain today where there is forestry surrounded by moorland or heath.

The first written references to the bird in relation to its opportunist habit of raiding crops are not found until the eighteenth century. This coincided with the change from the open field and common grazing, little altered since medieval times, to the enclosing of fields and introduction of root crops as winter cattle feed, which revolutionised the production of grain and meat. There are references to pigeon flocks feeding on these turnip tops in the winter, and later, with the advent of clover into the agricultural system, pigeons had a staple form of winter food. This would have enabled the population to increase rapidly as winter losses were reduced.

No doubt this started in particular areas of Britain and expanded with the spread of new agricultural practices. This pattern developed over about two centuries, with agricultural rotations and innovations as horses gave way to mechanical power in the twentieth century. Agriculture was a highly labour-intensive activity with most of those living in the country working on farms of small fields and mixed farming. It is probable that the woodpigeon population grew slowly in line with agricultural productivity and the controlling factor was winter food that was weather related. However, the situation changed with the introduction of winter oilseed rape as a break crop in the 1970s over the major arable region of Britain. With the vast acreage now grown from the South Coast to as far north as Invernesshire in Scotland, the pigeon has a nutritious and widely available food source in all but the harshest winter conditions, when it is covered by deep snow. It has been shown that pigeons do not just survive but thrive on winter rape leaves and come out of the winter in excellent condition without loss of weight. As a result, severe winters are no longer the controlling factor and the woodpigeon population is as high now as it has probably ever been. This has been further aided by predominantly milder winters over the past twenty or thirty years, in spite of shooting pressure being greater than ever.

Shooting as a method of control

Increased food production and a burgeoning woodpigeon population have led to a greater need for crop protection and an increase in the number of people interested in shooting them. Sporting writers of the eighteenth and nineteenth centuries, while talking of large bags of game or wildfowl, rarely mentioned woodpigeon in their game diaries, let alone actually setting out to shoot them. Therefore we can assume that there were not great numbers at that time and pigeons that did threaten crops were chased off by men and boys with bird-scaring rattles. The twentieth century, however, was different, and there are many reports of keepers or sportsmen focusing on shooting the bird for crop protection and sport.

Since the 1950s Major Archie Coats, operating mainly in Hampshire and Berkshire, was possibly the first professional pigeon shooter. He later became my guide and guru but more of that in later chapters. His book *Pigeon Shooting*, published in 1963, became a classic and an inspiration to many who have become enthusiastic pigeon shooters over the years.

The fact was that, in the twentieth century, the woodpigeon population had become a serious threat to food production. This was recognised

BACKGROUND INFORMATION

officially and addressed by post-war politicians when food was in short supply and rationed. Following a report by the Ministry of Agriculture's scientist, M.K. Colquhoun, the Ministry introduced a scheme whereby approved pigeon shots were supplied with half-price cartridges. This was an addition to the subsidy on cartridges for shooting rabbits, another species in great numbers destroying crops before the introduction of myxomatosis. The resulting scheme was the formation of rabbit clearance societies (RCSs). These were set up all over Britain where rabbits and pigeons were a problem. Of course the cheap cartridge scheme was, at times, abused but it was at least recognition at government level of the bird as a serious agricultural pest and shooting as an effective method of control. The RCSs died a death as funds dried up but the principle has remained and is the reason why the woodpigeon can be shot throughout the year under general licences.

General licences

These general licences are discussed in detail in Appendix 1, but in brief the position is this. The woodpigeon was one of a number of pest species that could be shot throughout the year as a provision of the 1981 Wildlife and Countryside Act. All good common sense, so far. However, in 1990 the interfering bureaucrats in Brussels decreed that Britain was not complying with the terms of the 1979 Birds Directive, which stipulated that no birds could be shot during the breeding season. This was perhaps sensible in the European countries where pigeons were in modest numbers and did not threaten crops, but the UK has a high pigeon population and so both the National Farmers Union (NFU), the agricultural voice and the BASC, the voice of shooting, lobbied hard for a compromise that, in Britain, we could shoot pigeons throughout the year to protect crops from woodpigeon damage. The campaign was successful and, under an EU derogation, the UK administration can issue general licences that are renewed annually and sanctioned by Brussels.

Though a sensible compromise in my view, it is still subject to an annual review and this has the frailty of becoming more political and less practical in the eyes of those responsible for reviewing the licence. Maybe I am becoming over-cynical as I spend many thinking hours in a pigeon hide protecting summer crops.

BASC Woodpigeon Working Group

It became clear that, if the licence was ever to become a contentious issue, then good statistics should be to hand. In 1992 the BASC began a successful programme of research in co-operation with The Game Conservancy (now Game and Wildlife Conservation Trust), NFU and MAFF (Ministry of Agriculture, Fisheries and Food, now Defra). Also included in the group were pigeon shooting representatives from each area of Britain, of which I was the East Anglian member. The result of this study was based on facts emanating from questionnaires sent to all BASC members (111,000 at that time). Many good statistics were the positive result and the BASC is still very active in monitoring woodpigeon shooting and helping members to protect crops and enjoy the sport while doing so.

Effectiveness of shooting as a method of control

Shooting is recognised by Defra as the most effective form of controlling woodpigeons feeding on agricultural crops. This is obvious as pigeons shot do not come back to eat more crops, nor do they breed. Farmers have an arsenal of deterrents including gas guns, rope bangers, kites, polythene flags or regularly having staff on patrols firing shots to disturb feeding birds. There are now devices which broadcast calls of birds of prey. All these forms of deterrent have one thing in common – they do not kill the birds, they just, at best, move them. What is worse is that these methods encourage them to flock up and so make it more difficult for the pigeon shooter to get the opportunity to shoot numbers of them as, if a flock comes into the decoys, the maximum number killed can only relate to the number of shots fired. For one man with a double-barrelled gun, that is two. The result is two dead at best and maybe a hundred frightened off to another field to continue damaging crops.

However it is the birds' habit to flock in winter and so it is not until the late spring that these flocks break up and birds fly in ones, twos or small parties to feed. It is therefore not surprising that around 80% of the total bag of pigeons are shot on crops from March to November. These are exactly the months proposed as a closed season if the general licence was ever revoked. Therefore only 20% would be shot in the open season in winter and the only successful method of control would be severely reduced in Britain.

So how many are shot, you may well ask? A simple question, but with no easy answer, as figures suggested vary so greatly that the exact figure could never be known. But if I had to guess I would suggest between four and six million. However, what is more certain is that the population is increasing according to two sources of independent figures, the British Trust of Ornithology (BTO) who run The Breeding Bird Survey (BBS) and the RSPB winter garden bird count.

BACKGROUND INFORMATION

The sceptic may then say that, if these statistics show the woodpigeon population to be increasing, then shooting is not a successful control of the bird's population. However I would argue that this is not true. The total number of birds shot represents a significant percentage of the population, which is being contained successfully by shooting. Every area of Britain where pigeons are found is being shot by someone. The number of enthusiastic pigeon shooters is growing and over most of the country there is not a field where pigeons are feeding that will not be shot within a day or two. That will reduce a percentage of birds feeding on the field. As those surviving birds go on to feed on another field another percentage will be shot and so on. Over a year, a group of pigeon shooters in an area will have a definite effect and shooting birds before the breeding season will contain the autumn population.

Ethics of summer shooting

This raises the question of shooting pigeons during their breeding season. Actually, as eggs are laid and young fledge in every month of the year, one could ask when is not their breeding season? Obviously, in summer, a bird shot is more likely to have a nest and none of us would like to think of the squabs being deprived of food. However there are two good reasons why it is not such a problem. First, the emotional concern is eased by the fact that only one bird of the pair flies out to feed at a time, while the other remains to brood or protect the nest from predators. Therefore the young may not be orphaned. Second, the reason why general licences are in place is to prevent crop damage. The farmer sees pigeons on his fields as he views rats in his barn – a problem. He would not be pleased if, when he called a pest officer to poison his rats and mice, the man said he would not come now because they might be suckling young!

However, summer shooting is a sensitive subject and must be a personal decision, though do not be too surprised if you find someone else shooting on the farm later in the year if you declined to go on the farmer's peas or laid wheat when he phoned you in June or July. Personally I love and admire the woodpigeon as a bird and as a sporting quarry. However, I do respect the farmer's attitude and it is his crop and livelihood that are threatened and, in the bigger picture, he is producing the food on which an ever-growing population is dependent. It would be a frail argument to a Third World country who might want our surplus to feed their starving millions if our government official had to report 'Sorry, no surplus this year as the pigeons ate it while pigeon shooters gave the birds time to breed'. This may be an

extreme example to make a point, but who knows? The fact is that pigeons do eat a serious tonnage of corn despite being shot throughout the summer. The other fact is that the pigeon population is not declining but growing, so if one parent is shot it is likely that the other parent successfully rears the one or two squabs in the nest. So, maybe we are being over-emotional; Nature is more than holding her own.

If, however, there comes a time in the future when, for whatever reason, the pigeon population seriously declines, then there would be a reason to reconsider both on a personal level and a national conservation level. But while suitable nesting habitat is increasing and agricultural cropping produces abundant food for the birds throughout the year, that situation is unlikely (though there is always the possibility that Nature herself might intervene when the population becomes too high and reduce it with an avian disease).

Breeding habits of the woodpigeon

You may wonder why we have not looked at the nesting and breeding habits of the bird earlier in the book, following a description of the bird as you might have expected. However, as lack of winter food no longer controls the population the greatest impact is made by predation on nests and limited food supply for the young. Therefore it is appropriate to look in detail now at the demographics of the bird's distribution and annual population fluctuations.

The woodpigeon can nest throughout the year and young can fledge in every month. Though a flock bird in winter, it is territorial in its nesting habit. Interestingly, it is basically a social bird and its territory is established in a rather gentlemanly fashion without resorting to violent conflict (as does the pheasant, for example). The pigeon arrangement is more like people arriving on a beach on a summer's day. The first arrivals set up deckchairs far apart. Then, as more and more families arrive they fill in the gaps, still observing the furthest distance from previous arrivals. Then yet more people occupy those spaces and so on, until everyone is happy to sit right next to one another. I'm not suggesting pigeons end up like rooks, cheek by jowl on the same tree, but in prime habitat where the population is high they will happily nest within ten to twenty yards of each other.

To establish territories the birds will coo in their delightful way 'coo – cooo – coo – coo – coo' – repeated several times but ending in a short 'coo'. This calming, almost soporific, sound of summer in any woodland or garden is gently telling other males that this is their patch. Interestingly, the cooing

BACKGROUND INFORMATION

pigeon does not open its beak but coos through its nose. It is therefore a form of nasal humming. I have even heard them doing this in total darkness, at 11.30 p.m. in March when three individual birds were cooing in turn from their favourite trees about a hundred yards apart.

The courtship begins with the male bowing his head as he moves closer to the female. She will then engage in what is the nearest thing to kissing as the two birds lovingly entwine beaks from side to side. This is usually followed by mating. This only takes place when she is ready and he may have been previously chasing her around on the ground or in the trees making his intentions clear, but with her being equally clear as she rebuffed his advances. What's new in the lives of birds or humans? Another common courtship display is the unusual flight as birds rise in the air, clap their wings and descend. This is repeated in a rhythmic progression; one bird follows the other like a slow motion roller-coaster.

Display Flight

If a confrontation occurs on the edge of territories it is again resolved in a chivalrous way. I have watched two males on an electricity line sitting only about ten feet from each other, then one started to sidestep towards the second. This was permitted until an invisible line was crossed, at which time the second bird sidestepped towards the chap who had overstepped the mark and went along until he nudged the first bird back in the direction of his own patch. A flutter of the first bird and he went back to sit as before, ten feet from the second bird who had, himself, sidestepped back. Peace was restored but the whole charade was repeated from time to time. I suspect this usually takes place hidden by leaves as the birds sit on a branch of a tree on the boundary of two territories.

A pigeon's territory needs the right bushy trees or hedge in which to build a nest, and to be within easy flight of a food source and also, importantly, water. Pigeons drink in an unusual way and, unlike most species which dip their beaks into water before raising their head and tilting it back to allow the water to run down their throat, the pigeon can use its bill to suck like a straw without raising its head.

The nest is in low scrub, a hedge or woodland, usually between ten and thirty feet from the ground. In large blocks of forestry or woodland, nests are usually around the edges. Small woods and hedgerows are favoured habitats but, since the end of the nineteenth century, with the increase in urbanisation, towns have produced perfect nesting territories and habitat.

The Nest

With the ever-growing suburban fringe to every town a mosaic of suitable trees, hedges and tall shrubs around lawns, flower beds and vegetable gardens has made, perhaps, the best possible nesting habitat – the equivalent to woodland with a million glades. As one flies over a town and looks down, there is more greenery than building in the suburbs. Ponds provide water and gardens supply natural as well as bird table supplementary feed for a bird which, after all, originally dwelt in the primeval forests of Britain and only later exploited arable farmland. So, while those people living in suburbs or villages may not like the analogy of primeval forest, our man-made environment is close to that habitat originally supporting the 'wood' pigeon.

BACKGROUND INFORMATION

The pigeon's nest is an open, flat raft of small twigs about a foot in diameter. Those built in conifers are more hidden but those in deciduous trees or hedges are very visible to humans, let alone predators. Interestingly, the birds are very particular about the twigs used and I have observed both birds of a pair carefully selecting those twigs which had blown off a tree, each one being picked up by one end and then, with the other end on the ground, being subjected to a test of springiness. If it broke it was discarded as too brittle. This may explain why many twigs are broken off live trees despite this requiring considerable effort. The more one observes the bird the more fascinating and different it is from other species.

The hen lays only two white eggs, which sit on the flat nest in full view from above and, unless protected by a parent, would appear as breakfast, lunch or tea served on a plate to any magpie, jay, crow or grey squirrel. Both sexes incubate the eggs and keep to a daily routine in which the male is on the eggs from around 10.00 a.m. until 4.00 p.m. while the female goes off to feed. She returns and incubates for the other eighteen of the twenty-four hours (Murton). If food is short, the sitting bird may leave the nest early, or the other return late. This leads to predation of the unguarded nest.

These spring and early summer nests are offering eggs at the time the predators are themselves feeding young and so have an increased demand for food. It is therefore hardly surprising that up to 90% of early nests fail. The exception to this is on estates with intensive keepering, where wild game is the priority. The control of corvids and squirrels by trapping or shooting will enable these eggs to hatch. However, the next problem for early-hatched young is for the parent birds to find enough nutritious food at that time of year. It was shown by Dr Ron Murton on the Carlton Study Area of East Cambridgeshire that adults followed the same strict timetable when brooding as when incubating.

The young hatch after seventeen days of incubation. A squab, as a young pigeon is called, is not the most beautiful of chicks – not the cute little Easter chick or attractive baby duckling. No, it is a naked, rather bald little creature with a few hairs and a disproportionately large beak to receive the strange, soft, cheesy 'milk' from its parents as they insert their bills down the squab's throat.

This milk is produced from glands that develop on the inside of the crop of both parents. These are clearly visible if a crop of a parent bird is examined, appearing as a soft, white, crinkly rubbery lining. The milk produced is high in protein and easily digested by the young squabs to boost fast growth. Murton's research showed that the young are fed only the milk for the first three days, then 49% for the first seven to nine days, 33% until the tenth to

fourteenth day and thereafter 20% until the young fledge. The rest of the diet is from regurgitated food.

The young squabs' growth rate varies considerably dependent on the nutritional content of the food available. Cereals are particularly important to provide this quality of feed. In practice this means that birds of the spring and early summer broods, when cereals are not yet available, can take up to thirty-three or thirty-four days to fledge. However, those hatched from July to October are heavier at any age and can fledge in only sixteen to twenty days (Murton 1965). Furthermore, 60% of young that hatch early will die of malnutrition before July. Therefore, with the two factors of predation of eggs and malnutrition of hatched young, the result is that only a small percentage of young produced prior to July will reach adulthood.

There are exceptions, as with every generalisation, but these only occur in areas where there are few corvids and grey squirrels and ample nutritious food. I have seen this in the fertile East Anglian fens where one year a large area of chickweed produced flowers which pigeons came for miles to eat and, as early as June, there were many young on the wing. This can also be the case where early peas are grown that flower in late May and early June – these also produce the nutrition needed for young to be on the wing by the end of June. However, despite a good food source often being available early in the year, it is uncommon for a large percentage of young to survive before the end of June.

Now let us look at the optimum breeding period in July, August and September. By this time the mature foliage in woodland or hedgerows provides better cover for nests and hides the eggs from predators. The predators themselves are no longer feeding young with a high food demand and there is more food available in other forms.

This begins in June when wheat and barley ripen; then, from July onwards, there are the stubbles of winter rape, barley and wheat (obviously, timing varies across Britain and harvest in Scotland can be two months later than in the south). So easily gleaned cereals enable optimum growth and survival of the squabs. This in turn leads to fledging in little more than a fortnight and time for Mr and Mrs Pigeon to start another nest immediately. Therefore 70% of young flying at the end of the summer are from June, July and August nests. It is common for the bird to attempt to produce three broods in the year, and frequently more.

I have my own theory which I have never seen suggested by others. This is based on the observation that, in late spring and early summer, one still sees pigeons in groups and flocks flighting out to feed. These flocks are not as large as those seen in winter, but are not nesting birds which tend to flight

BACKGROUND INFORMATION

singly or in small groups. Therefore I feel these groups are birds from the late, previous summer broods which do not reach breeding condition until the following summer. So the previous year's young would also optimise their chances of success by joining in late summer nesting when food would be available for their young. This would further augment the late summer population of young. Ornithologically, most birds breed in their first year having been hatched in the spring of the previous year, although some large birds like geese do not reach breeding maturity until their second year. It seems biologically unlikely that a bird hatched late in the year will be mature enough to breed the following spring, when it may only be between five and seven months old. As I say, this is only my own theory, but I see a lot of evidence to support it.

Whether or not this is so, the fact is that by the end of the summer there is the highest number of young birds. Therefore, in September and October, there will be a high percentage of young in the bag. These are obvious by their smaller size and brown appearance, with no neck ring and no orange on the beak, which appears dull grey-brown. These birds are going to be less than six weeks old, at which age their first moult will produce the adult features.

At that time of year young birds might constitute up to 80% of the bag. But one should not assume that this reflects the true proportion of young to old of pigeons, as the young, inexperienced birds will decoy more readily and will not fly with the speed and agility of mature birds. It is at this time of year that, at the end of the day, I select the fattest young pigeons to prepare for the freezer as they make excellent eating (see Chapter 11 for tips on plucking and preparing pigeons for the table). They are so tender and delicious just roasted and compare well with any game bird.

The migration debate

So, at the end of the summer, large numbers of pigeons are feeding, mostly on stubbles which produce rich pickings and this abundant food ensures that the young birds from successful nests will develop and reach adulthood. Both they and the adults will put on fat for the winter. As stubbles disappear under the plough and winter drilled fields are cleared of seed on the surface, food will start to become more scarce. However, just as this happens the winter oilseed rape has grown to a size at which it is attractive to pigeons. This coincides with the time pigeons start to flock up for the winter, which is a natural phenomenon, partly to lead each other to the available food source of the day and partly as a protection from birds of prey. Peregrines

and sparrowhawks are the two main avian predators but the goshawk (which is rare in most parts of Britain) will readily take woodpigeons. Of the three species it is the sparrowhawk which is perhaps the most surprising, as it is no larger than a pigeon and, as its name suggests, it should mainly eat small birds. It would be all right if it selected only common birds like blue tits, but it takes any small bird and so is devastating to some rarer species. If one spotted flycatcher, lesser spotted woodpecker or whitethroat is taken then it leaves no chance for those birds breeding. The cuckoo used to be common and I feel that it, too, has suffered since, as each single youngster fledges, from whatever species' nest, it can be a focus as an easy meal for a sparrowhawk. However, although the woodpigeons taken will not significantly affect the population, being a large bird, it is not easily killed by a sparrowhawk and once caught is often brought to the ground to be plucked and eaten alive.

The limited work done on ringing woodpigeons indicates that a bird is rarely recovered more than twenty-five miles from where it was ringed. This suggests that there is only local movement. This, I am sure, is true of indigenous birds that live and nest in much of Britain, particularly those in the south. Squabs ringed in the nest will belong to the local static population. However, the work done is limited and I feel there is perhaps a larger picture.

It is certainly a fact that the woodpigeons of northern Europe migrate south and the population density is much lower in Europe, a fact borne out by the very modest bags ever shot there. However, when the birds from the vast area of northern Europe are funnelled through the Alps on their way south for the winter, the hourglass effect creates flocks of many thousands of birds. The French make a great feature of this *La Palombière* as a sport and hunting culture in autumn. They either shoot the birds as they fly over the high passes, or net them. To do so is not easy but there is a tradition that has evolved to achieve this successfully.

Hunters identify mountain valleys where the pigeons' main flight lines pass. Nets are rigged in the trees at the head of the valleys, but the birds are flying far too high to ever fly into them. The clever method devised to bring the birds down low is by using the birds' instinct to drive and gain speed if threatened by a bird of prey – of which there are many also migrating at that time of year. High platforms are strategically sited on the tops of either side of the valley. These are manned by experienced men who watch approaching flocks and, when the precise moment occurs, they throw out what looks like a white table tennis bat. This spins through the air above the migrating pigeons, which then dive to escape what they perceive to be a hawk or falcon and then fly at great speed up the valley hugging the ground. This then leads them into the net.

BACKGROUND INFORMATION

From the films I have seen this not only needs skilful bat throwers but also an element of luck. However it can be successful. The whole event is something of a ritual and party as those involved go up to the mountains for days and live in communal cabins while they wait for the right conditions for the migration. There appeared in the films to be a lot of time waiting for the moment of action and this was passed eating and drinking the local wine! Great culinary dishes of woodpigeon were on the menu.

The other form of *La Palombière* is practised in the large oak woods of southern France, where the migrating flocks rest and feed on acorns on their way south. There is the same camaraderie but, from the central cabin, there are a number of tunnels created with camouflaged netting. When pigeons arrive and sit in the trees the Guns creep through the tunnels to allotted trees where, on a signal, all shoot together and hope to kill a bird or two each. Both forms of *La Palombière* are very important seasonal events for each locality.

So, migration of woodpigeons on the Continent is a fact and is necessary because the northern countries experience severe winters and there might be no food for months to support the pigeon population. In Britain we have a more equable climate and so, although hard weather is experienced, there are acorns, beech mast and stubbles, with oilseed rape grown as far north as Inverness. Therefore pigeons do not have to migrate in the same way as in mainland Europe. However, there is considerable evidence of some movement south in winter from Scotland and northern Britain. There have also been many eye-witnessed occurrences of large flocks coming into East Anglia from the North Sea. Traditionally, the flocks have been spoken of as 'they foreigners' and described as being smaller and browner than the normal woodpigeon. This would, in fact, indicate that, whether indigenous or migrant, they were flocks containing many young birds. These large flocks, sometimes of several thousand birds, travel south-west through England and have then been witnessed by the BTO migration specialist, Paul Stancliffe, flying out to sea from the Dorset coast, obviously on their way to Brittany on migration to southern France and the Iberian peninsula.

Personally I feel that the main winter pigeon population of East Anglia comprises local birds that have flocked up plus some pigeons that instinctively move south and other Continental birds that drift across from northern Europe. Why does this not fit with the limited British ringing results? Possibly because those birds ringed in southern Britain do not need to move far, let alone migrate. I suspect very few pigeons have ever been ringed in northern Europe so we cannot identify migrating birds for certain. Until there is more extensive ringing of pigeons no conclusive statistical evidence will appear.

CHAPTER 3
YOUR GUN AND CARTRIDGES

Choosing and using your gun

Any gun with which you are comfortable and enjoy shooting will be suitable to shoot woodpigeons. There is nothing mythical about this and so if you are a clay shot your choice will usually be an over-and-under and if a game shot maybe a side-by-side. The key factor is that it must fit you and be of a weight you can mount easily and consistently. There are a number of factors affecting the fit of a gun including the length of the stock, the 'cast' (which is the deviation left or right of a line central to the barrel alignment) and 'drop' which is the angle of the ridge or comb of the stock. A good shooting instructor at any shooting ground can advise when they check your gun mount and see you shoot. It can all sound complicated but the fact is simple: when mounted, the barrel of the gun must be an extension of your eye. This will mean that, when fired, it will shoot at the point of aim. This can be checked by an instructor or by using a pattern plate. At home it is easily done by mounting the gun on fixed points in the room – maybe the door handle for low birds or the light fitting for higher ones. Ensure that you have ample room for this or the light bulb can suffer! Another very good check is to raise your gun to your own right eye (presuming you are right-handed) when standing in front of a mirror. You will immediately see if you are aiming to left or right, above or below your eye in the mirror. If all is well then test your swing by pretending a bird is perhaps flying along the picture rail or the line where the wall meets the ceiling. Then stop at the corner and close your left eye and check that you are on the mark. Playing 'gun ups' at home is a great way of practising your gun mounting, which must be consistent for every angle of shot.

YOUR GUN AND CARTRIDGES

Always ensure that your feet are positioned to allow the optimum amount of swing. This means, for a right-handed shot, when facing the point of aim that the left foot is pointing at about one o'clock and the right foot at three. This will mean your hips and shoulders will be at about 45° from the front. Try standing more square than this and you will find you cannot swing comfortably to your right without the gun rolling low off the line of the bird.

If standing correctly then the swing should start from the ground and come up through every level of joints: knees, hips to shoulders, so the well-mounted gun is part of the upper body, shoulders and head.

I had not meant this to turn into a shooting lesson but it is a fact that the gun, though it may be the finest in the world, is only as good as the person using it, whatever your target – clays, game or pigeons. There are many good books on how to shoot and there are shooting grounds with experienced instructors throughout the country. We can't all be world champions but we can all learn to shoot to the best of our ability, and can learn from the well-known story of the great golfer, Arnold Palmer. When someone said to Palmer that he was lucky to win so many tournaments, he answered profoundly: 'Yes, and the funny thing is that the more I practise the luckier I become.'

Pigeon shooting can produce both the easiest shot and the most difficult, all on the same day. The key thing is to enjoy it all and, above all, shoot safely.

So back to the type of gun: it really is a question of the one you enjoy and have confidence in using. Most people use 12 bore shotguns, but 20 bores can be just as effective. Some aficionados use 28 bores and even .410s, but unless you are a very good shot, it is sensible to reduce the range at which you shoot with such guns.

As to the relative merits of shooting a side-by-side or over-and-under, it is a personal choice. I have shot with side-by-sides for most of my life and love their balance and spontaneity. However, my Beesleys were made in 1907 and are beginning to have a few breakdowns as age takes its toll, rather like their owner. Nevertheless I like to keep them for game shooting and decided that I should use a modern gun for pigeons, made to take the sharper recoil of today's fast cartridges. I have therefore been using an over-and-under in recent years and so the bulk of cartridges fired in a year now go through this gun, which is built with the weight and strength to absorb fast cartridges of any load. Over-and-unders tend to be heavy and this aids a steady swing, which is good for longer birds. The single sight plane of stacked barrels makes it very pointable and better for long going-away shots. Therefore I have experience of both forms of gun and feel happy to shoot with either. For anyone starting to shoot I would recommend an over-and-under as they are easier to shoot; however the traditionalist will enjoy the sporting quality of a side-by-side. All will kill pigeons if pointed in the right direction.

The semi-automatic shotgun is a good tool for pigeon shooting as the third shot can be useful. However, when I have tried one there was seldom an opportunity for three shots and maybe I am old-fashioned, but feel that two shots at a bird is sporting, but not three! I also feel that a right-and-left with two shots is both pleasing to the shooter and effectively protects the crop. A problem with semi-automatics is that the ejected cartridge cases are thrown out in all directions and, as it is always important to pick up all spent cases at the end of the day, this can be difficult, especially in summer when the vegetation is thick and makes finding spent cases a problem.

There are semi-automatics fitted with sound-moderator barrels, which can be helpful if shooting either near a built-up area or in the vicinity of the woodland that is the background from where the pigeons are coming out to feed. In that situation birds will not be disturbed. Also, oncoming birds may be at a distance where a suppressed sound of a shot does not disturb them. Personally, however, when I tried one, I found it very ungainly to shoot. The sound-moderated barrel was very heavy and the gun so unbalanced that it was not only an effort to shoot but gave little pleasure as it was so awkward. I could, I'm sure, have got used to it in time and it would be an advantage on occasions, but I get so much pleasure from using a well-balanced gun that I am not convinced of its net benefits. If there was a way of sound-moderating my normal guns without changing their balance then I would opt for that. However, the sound of the shot can often help as it will prevent birds settling downwind on your field or in surrounding trees and hedges. They will normally fly upwind to your position if disturbed rather than disappearing away downwind.

I have not yet spoken about the best chokes for pigeon shooting. Shots at decoyed birds can be at close range, while others may be high or wide. Therefore it is ideal to have two barrels with appropriate chokes. Improved cylinder in the right barrel of a side-by-side and ½ or ¾ choke in the left barrel will produce a good combination. My over-and-

The gun in the 'ready' position for taking a shot.
(Rupert Watts)

YOUR GUN AND CARTRIDGES

under Kemen has not got a barrel selector and so it always fires the bottom barrel first. This has fixed chokes of ½ and ½. It is a bit tight for close birds but, on the whole, is good for everything, though I would prefer to be able to select either open or choke barrel.

I am not a techno-buff about guns or cartridges but have a practical approach, which is to concentrate on getting any shot from any gun in the right place to kill the pigeon. Pilot error is the main reason for a bird not being killed. However the authoritative Appendix 2 addresses the technical side of guns and explains in more detail the merits of features which will help you choose what is right for you.

Finally, if it looks like a big day it is a good idea to take a spare gun if you have one. Guns do break down occasionally and a spare locked up in the cabinet at home is of no use. If you do carry a spare it is recommended that it should be hidden in your locked car and, as an added security precaution, the fore-end should be removed and kept with you.

Cartridges

Here we enter the minefield of endless discussions between shooting folk, comparing such variables of cartridge make, load, shot size, wad type and – importantly for pigeon shooting – price. However, before going any further we must dismiss the myth that the woodpigeon is a tough bird that can carry a lot of shot. This misconception arises because if the shot does not kill but the outer pellets of the pattern pass through the feathers, a plume will be left drifting on the wind especially if, as is usual, it is missed behind. The bird is covered in loose feathers and one pellet can cut a swathe out of them. The result is that the bird may appear to have been hit hard when it has not. So the myth is born rather than accepting that the shot was missed or the bird wounded.

I used to load my own cartridges in my early days, when to do so was economical, and I tested shot sizes from 4s to 9s. They all killed pigeons but only if the lead was put in the right place. So, as I pointed out when discussing the choice of gun, the key emphasis should be on practice to put the shot in the right place to achieve consistent and clean kills. After all, we are out in the field to protect the farmer's crop and dead pigeons do not come back next day to do more damage. Two bangs and a miss may frighten the bird off, but it will be back eating crops tomorrow.

So what do we look for in the optimum cartridge for our choice of gun? It must carry a load heavy enough to kill pigeons but not so heavy that it is uncomfortable when you fire a lot of shots on a busy day. Over many years of pigeon shooting I feel that a 28g or 30g load is quite sufficient. There are people who use 32g or more. I once found a hide where there were 36g cases on the ground. Of course, they should have been collected up and taken home but maybe the chap's shoulder was too painful and his headache so severe he forgot! Heavy loads are needed for very high pheasants or long-range wildfowl but not for general pigeon shooting.

The shot size chosen needs to be a compromise between being large enough to have punch but small enough to produce a pattern density to ensure enough pellets strike the bird. I find that in most situations a shot size of 6 to 7½ will kill consistently. If one were to pluck a pigeon and hang it up forty yards away it would look very small, and actually the body is no larger than a clay pigeon. However, though forty to fifty yards is a long range, it is well within the capabilities of modern cartridges. So there must be enough pellets to create a sufficient pattern and in recent years I have found that 28g which contains 385 pellets of 7½ shot produces the optimum compromise. If using a 30g load, then No.7 shot will create a similar pattern and be equally effective. The two loads, if using No.6 shot, would have 270 pellets in a 28g cartridge and 287 in one of 30g. This reduces the pattern by more than 25%. For a bird as small as a pigeon I think this is more relevant than the reduction of size of shot from No.6 at 2.6mm diameter to No.7½ shot at 2.3mm. However, that is only my personal opinion and the more important point, science or no science, is to put whatever shot is used in the right place to achieve clean kills.

Perhaps I should explain that I am lucky to fire more shots than most people at pigeons and have done for many years, shooting 5,000–6,000 in fifty to sixty days decoying. About ten years ago I developed a shoulder and neck stiffness. This I attributed to the fact that I shoot up to 7,500 cartridges a year from a sitting position and this precludes the recoil from being taken through my body and therefore it is all dissipated in my upper body. As this did not happen when standing to shoot game in the winter my theory was sufficiently proven to act upon it. I therefore bought two heavy side-by-sides built in 1907 as live pigeon guns. In the days before clay pigeons, there were competitions using live birds, which involved large wagers and the participants used guns of increased weight to absorb the recoil of the heavy loads that were used to ensure clean kills. This was because a bird was only counted if it fell within a certain radius of the boxes from which the feral pigeons were sprung. So, for me, these side-by-side boxlocks with 32-inch barrels and weighing 7lb 12oz were very substantial and more like the competition over-and-unders of today. The key element was that the extra weight absorbed most of the recoil and, when combined with a light 28g load, it solved my recoil problem when shooting pigeons, seated in a hide. Many clay shots have similar problems as they fire great numbers of cartridges in practice or competition. I do not want to bore you with my personal physical problems but simply recount this story as a warning to be careful and aware of the importance of the relationship between gun and cartridge over a period of time, and its consequences. (While on health issues don't forget to always wear hearing protection. I will talk about plugs or muffs later.)

If you shoot a lot of pigeons you will want to look out for the best offers on cartridges as, with the ever-spiralling cost of lead combined with the increase in other components, cartridges have increased enormously in price and little change is foreseeable. It can also pay to combine with friends to order in bulk and possibly negotiate a discount.

The brand of cartridge is less important than it was years ago, as today all manufacturers have to produce top-quality products. This has been driven by the volume production of the clay world, wherein no manufacturer of poor cartridges would stay in business. For most of the twentieth century Eley had something of a monopoly and the Impax 1oz loads and Grand Prix 30g were the standard cartridges available. Then, some foreign cartridges were imported and these were much cheaper – though they had some strange habits, at times creating smoke, flames and confetti as wads disintegrated – and they kicked like the proverbial mule. Not surprisingly these did not last and other British and European manufacturers saw the opportunity to develop top-quality clay competition and club cartridges. Most manufacturers now produce a full range of cartridges aimed at the clay and game market, and a derivative as a load for pigeon shooters. Economical pigeon cartridges are often based on one of the high-volume production lines of clay cartridges, where the machines are efficiently producing 24/7. This is helpful and the pigeon shooter is therefore well served by top-quality cartridges made for the clay world and shares in the competitive price.

A final word on cartridges: always put more in the car than you think you may need. Most of those who shot record bags ran out of cartridges. Records we do not need as an ambition, however there are already enough problems in creating a good day's pigeon shooting and running out of cartridges does not need to be one of them.

Always remember to clear up your empties at the end of the day and leave the countryside as you found it.

For more technical data see Appendix 2. This was produced by Dr John Harradine, Director of Research at the BASC.

CHAPTER 4
WHAT KIT DO YOU NEED?

This is an important chapter. Over the years I have acquired various pieces of equipment which are either important in helping to get a day's shooting underway from the start or to help me be more comfortable for what can often be long hours in the hide. It is interesting that Archie Coats, in his authoritative book *Pigeon Shooting*, had no chapter at all on the equipment he used. However, although he dismissed the subject by saying he had just a gun, cartridges, hide poles and nets, a few dead birds in a sack and a five-gallon oil drum to sit on, he did in fact think more carefully than he acknowledged about the sort of poles, nets, decoys and kit he actually used. There are a number of traps along the way for a beginner and a confusing array of equipment on sale, some vital but some gismos less so. It is rather like fishing flies – some catch more fisherman than fish!

However, equipment does not have to be complicated or expensive. I have, at times, had no pigeon shooting kit with me and have seen pigeons feeding on a field while away painting commissions. Having got permission from the farmer and a borrowed a gun and cartridges, I have improvised to shoot a good bag of pigeons. Perhaps before talking in detail about the components of what is often a car-full of kit I will briefly tell the story of one such day as an example.

I was painting a landscape on the River Tweed when I observed a line of pigeons crossing my view all morning. At lunchtime I ate my sandwiches while parked in the gateway of a stubble field near to where the pigeons were flighting. Actually there were three good flight lines coming to the field and an encouraging number of birds feeding on the ground. The owner of the estate coincidentally stopped for a chat that afternoon when I was back at my easel and kindly said it would be fine for me to shoot next day. I was staying nearby with my cousin, and her husband lent me a gun and a bag of cartridges.

WHAT KIT DO YOU NEED?

The following day I arrived and watched the field again to select the spot in the hedgerow crossed by the main line of incoming birds. It was easy to break a few branches to make a hide and I had my folding painting chair for a comfortable seat. I shot a bird or two as they came from behind over my left shoulder and immediately set them up as decoys with a twig under their chins. Soon the two became four and then I was away as birds decoyed and compound interest created a full picture of dead birds. From that point it was just good sport until the evening when I picked up, having started with the bare minimum of equipment. I kept a few birds for my cousin to produce a good meal. The rest of the bag of a hundred I gave to the keeper on the estate for him to sell to his game dealer and so he had a drink out of my enjoyment of good sport on his beat; everyone was happy.

I wish all days were that easy but now that we know you are happy with your gun and cartridges let us look in detail at the additional kit that may be needed to make a successful day.

Let's assume we are loading up the car from the pigeon shed with all the kit possibly required for the day. You are coming out to shoot with me using my equipment and have just your gun and cartridges. *Always remember cartridges.* My nightmare of Hell in the next life would be a place with a million pigeons, a beautiful gun, but no cartridges. My old friend, Archie Coats, had a day like that on one occasion. In his latter years, when he was disabled, his ever-patient wife Prue would go out with him. She would build his hide, put out his seat, set up the decoys and then go home to get on with domestic chores. This day, all day, pigeons arrived from every point of the compass to come to his decoys but all Archie could do was watch as the cartridges were still in the Land Rover back at home. There were no mobile phones in those days so Archie could but rant and rave until Prue arrived to pick him up at the end of the day. Not a moment of marital bliss I suspect!

Vehicle

There is no doubt about it, you really do need a 4x4 to go pigeon shooting regularly. Otherwise there is a lot of walking, carrying kit out to shoot and hopefully a sack or two of birds to carry off the field at the end of the day. In dry weather a car will be fine across stubble and around farm tracks – if they are not too rutted. However the options are considerably extended if you are in a 4x4 with higher ground clearance than a car and good traction; you can then get to otherwise inaccessible places and save a lot of hard work. Even with a 4x4 you still have plenty of exercise carrying kit where the crops prevent getting any closer to the selected spot for a hide. It is all good character-building stuff and after fifty years of it I am still driven by enthusiasm and excitement to hike out miles into a field of peas if it is the right place to go, even though nowadays it may take two journeys when in my younger days I would stagger out in one.

Kit in my vehicle for a day decoying pigeons.

1. Canvas windbreak for back of hide
2. Flags
3. Rotary
4. Camouflage netting
5. Umbrella
6. Gun and sleeve
7. Hide poles
8. Dead pigeon decoys
9. Swivel chair
10. Bag of artificial decoys
11. Scott
12. Dog water and bowl
13. Cradles
14. Flapper
15. Travel bag containing small items
16. Loppers
17. Cartridges
18. Bow saw
19. Warm camo coat
20. Spade

Binoculars

These are essential and it is wise to invest in the best you can afford. They do not need to be expensive but I would recommend buying a good second-hand pair rather than a cheap new pair, whatever your budget. This policy provides the best lenses for the cash expended and then you do not have to treat them quite so carefully. They are there to do a job and mine are a good second-hand pair which are in my car, permanently out of their case, ready for use whenever, wherever. They are an essential piece of equipment for reconnaissance as it is often best to view a field or area of farmland from a distance.

Hide poles

In my early days I used hazel sticks cut from a wood in Hampshire. Each was about five feet long with a V at the top. They were very light to carry and lasted for years. However, there are now many makes of good telescopic poles on the market for hide building. Whether you buy two- or three-section poles will depend on space in your vehicle and whether they are to be carried in a bag. I prefer the three section ones, which provide more options, and I have a bunch of five held together top and bottom with elastic bungees. Five are better than four as they give greater flexibility to the shape of a hide and, on windy days, it is better to have three at the back to brace against the breeze. Hide poles are generally sold in sets of four, so you may need to make an extra one of an ash or hazel stick after all.

It is important that they have strong kicker plates and strong spikes to go into the soil. If the ground is hard it will take a lot of welly to get them solid. If not made of strong alloy they will break.

The tops are usually made with an easy clasp or V-shaped; either is good. The telescopic joints can be either rubber or plastic compression push joints or involve plastic rings with screw button tighteners. These are good on a windy day as the button is useful as an extra fixing point for the camouflage netting which the poles support.

Rucksack and bag

You will need something in which to load the day's equipment when a hide is not accessible by vehicle. The larger the better, and for years I have used an old army kitbag. This has a spacious capacity and comfortable shoulder straps. However if I had to start again I think I would look for a modern large rucksack, as it would be useful to have side pockets as well as the capacity to carry nets, cartridges, decoys, etc. Also modern rucksacks have a back support and front strap to make the load more comfortable to carry and probably better for reducing strain on your back.

Ensure that your rucksack is strong enough to carry a heavy load of cartridges, dead bird decoys and maybe a battery for your rotary. A good tip is to wait until your local camping or outdoor centre has a sale, when a good bargain can often be achieved. Every High Street has a travel shop or ex-army store. However, do ensure that whatever you buy is well made so that it will last many outings.

In addition to my army kitbag I used to have an old game bag in which I carried the many small bits and pieces needed. However, I now use a small travel bag with a shoulder strap and pockets with zip fasteners, which is better as items can be kept in their own compartments.

One sees combination bags which also act as a seat. These can work for some people and can be a useful way of solving two problems in one. Only time will tell what you personally find is the best solution, as no two pigeon shooters seem to carry their kit in the same way.

Camouflaged nets

In the old days there was but one version of this, which was the ex-army type. This was a string net of square holes inter-woven with strips of hessian. Each net comprised three colours, brown, dark green and natural hessian sack colour. They worked well but on a rainy day became very wet and heavy. Modern technology has now produced some very light screen netting in good patterns and colours that are lighter to carry, and pack into a compact space. They are available in two or three shades of green which are ideal for use all through the summer. However, later in the summer when shooting on rape or cereal stubbles, and when the hedgerow grasses have died, a desert form of camo net is useful.

For winter, when hedgerows are bare, there are nets of greys and browns or mixed camo patterns available. To collect a selection for all occasions is sensible and I carry two or three in my bag, but this is not strictly necessary as the camo net is only the basis of your hide, which is ideally then covered with natural vegetation. This should be chosen from your surroundings, e.g. hedge or tree branches if you are on the edge of woodland or in a hedge, and maybe the straw of any stubble if the hide is out in the field.

WHAT KIT DO YOU NEED?

An important point, which may be based more on my sensitivity with the eye of an artist, is that the tone of the nets used should be neither too dark nor too light compared with the background cover. We will talk about hide construction later but camo nets are a very important part of one's equipment, as to keep well hidden from oncoming pigeons is secondary only to keeping still.

It may sound odd but for years I have used an old piece of the ex-army netting which has lost all its interwoven hessian strips, having first faded in the sunlight and then become old and brittle until they sort of moulted and were shed like feathers of a bird. This bare grey-brown string net is used double along the top of my hide and makes a perfect screen through which to see but without being seen. It just breaks up my shape but produces an ideal top six inches for vision.

Clear-view scrim netting is also very clever as one can see out quite clearly but birds cannot see in. The only problem with modern light nets is that on windy days they can move and flap about unless well attached to your hide poles. Clamp clips can be useful to prevent this.

A variety of different colours of camouflaged netting for use as appropriate throughout the year.

Seat

Some may like to stand in a hide all day but this can be tiring. Others make cramped hides in ditches and kneel like wildfowlers, which is fine for an hour or so for a morning or evening flight on the marsh, but for five or six hours waiting for pigeons it is extremely uncomfortable. Archie Coats introduced me to the five-gallon steel drum as a seat. If lucky, one was also given a sorbo-rubber cushion and it was important to check that the drum's rim had been hammered down, otherwise it cut into the back of one's upper legs or backside. This form of seat was easily carried, having a loop of binder twine through the handle of the drum. However respectful I was of my hero, it later occurred to me that there must be more comfortable forms of seat. So a long evolution has taken place from a kitchen chair with the back broken off to a wooden chair with a high back found on a skip in the road. This, my old shooting pal and well-known writer, the late John Humphreys, referred to as the 'Chippendale'. Certainly a chair with a back is more comfortable.

Then came another development in the shape of a heavy swivelling secretary's chair, also found on a skip. This literally revolutionised my shooting in a hide whilst ensuring my comfort. This is because I usually sit to shoot and, with this type of chair, I could swivel round 360°, equating to footwork when standing for game shooting. However, though this old swivel chair was strong, made of sturdy steel, it was impractically heavy to lug out with my kit to the middle of a field or far hedgerow. Eventually I accepted that, for a modest investment, I could purchase a modern lightweight version from a commercial stationery office supplier. These chairs do not last more than two years but actually, in my case, that is about one hundred outings and for about £25 they are worth every penny. So, after fifty years of pigeon shooting I am a little wiser and a lot more comfortable.

Game shots going pigeon decoying for the first time usually arrive with a traditional shooting stick seat. This is all right perhaps for roost shooting, but is not stable enough in a pigeon hide unless it is the three-legged tripod type, which is fine at first but uncomfortable after several hours.

An office-type swivel chair is comfortable and allows for easy 360° movement. (Don Brunt)

Decoys

Decoys are, of course, an essential requirement to attract pigeons within range when shooting from a hide. There are two types, 'natural' and 'artificial'.

Naturals

A natural dead bird is the best decoy by far. No decoy can look more like a woodpigeon than the real thing and there is no doubt about it. Pigeons themselves know it and experienced pigeon shooters do also. The catch twenty-two question is how do you get dead pigeons to start with? Obviously those who are out regularly can hold some birds back from the game dealer, but that is only possible in the cool weather of winter. However, the easy way to solve the problem is to keep some in your freezer. Ideally this should be a chest freezer and used only for storage of your shot birds (more about this later) and a basket of those kept for decoys. To try this in the freezer compartment of a fridge in your kitchen is unlikely to be a popular move unless you live alone. If you are married and try it you may soon find you *are* living alone!

The key thing is that nothing is as good as a dead bird decoy. However, there are ways of achieving the nearest to best thing. One is to preserve by, in effect, stuffing some well-conditioned birds selected from a day's bag. WAGBI, the organisation which evolved to become the BASC, pioneered a method of doing this. It involves parting the breast feathers and easing back the skin before cutting the breastbone at the shoulder wing joints. The meat is then lifted out on the breastbone shield (and saved for a meal). Next, clean out the gut and swab out the body cavity with formaldehyde. You must wear rubber gloves for this procedure as the formaldehyde is a 40% solution of formalin which will in effect pickle any flesh – so do not let it touch yours. This solution is injected with a syringe into the wing joints, head and tail section. A piece of wire of suitable length is then inserted into the skull and tail section to support the shape of the bird. The body cavity is then stuffed with kapok and the skin sewn up. This was a rough way of setting up the bird but, as it was only to be seen by the pigeons from above, the breast did not have to be a work of taxidermist's art. I used to do this, although it took quite a long time and was a messy, fiddly job and could be dangerous if you were not protected. The resulting set of decoys was carried in a cardboard wine box with string handles. This protected the somewhat fragile decoys and they would last up to two years provided they did not get wet too often. However I lost one set to moths which caused the preserved bone, skin and feathers to disintegrate. I only tell of this process for interest and do not necessarily recommend it.

Plastic decoy with wings and tail of a real pigeon to make it more natural.

What I do suggest instead is the next best thing, which is to cover an artificial decoy with the wings and tail from a real pigeon. First, cut off the pair of wings at the shoulder joint. Then arrange these in a closed position on a metal tray and put them in the oven overnight at a low temperature. This is not popular with my wife, the queen of the kitchen, but I get away with it once every two years or so. The small amount of meat on a wing is thus dried to a point of preservation. The next step is to liberally cover the back and tail of an artificial decoy – the type does not matter – with glue. Copydex is good for this. Then, having plucked the tail feathers from a pigeon, stick two or three along the top of the tail and the wings on the back of the decoy, so that they meet across the middle of the back.

The result is a decoy of which only the head is not covered with natural pigeon feathers. When viewed from above, as it will be by pigeons flying over the field, 90% of what they see of each decoy is natural feathers. Again, these do last well if carried carefully and a light travel bag seems to work well for this.

Artificials

Now let us look at some of the various types of artificial decoy. The choice is considerable, as you will see advertised in every shooting magazine or offered for sale in gun shops and country fairs. With the ever-increasing popularity of woodpigeon shooting, the birds are naturally becoming more

WHAT KIT DO YOU NEED?

wary. In every area of Britain that has a woodpigeon population they are being shot to protect the farmer's crops and provide the shooter with sport in doing so. There are few areas where there are virgin adult pigeons that have not been offered decoys on one field or another and so decoys have to look very real. This is why dead birds are increasingly the most successful decoy to use. Artificials have to be very lifelike, or experienced birds will just turn away without presenting a shot.

The purpose of any artificial decoy is to start the ball rolling and as soon as any pigeons are shot it is best to build up the pattern of decoys with the real thing, the dead birds.

There are two main types of artificial, the 'shell' form which stack easily one into another or the 'full-bodied' decoy. The shells are easy to carry in a bag as a dozen or more just make a single compact bundle. They are good and work well but, whilst being light to carry, they can be *so* light that they blow about on a windy day. They come with a plastic support which, in a breeze, will allow the decoy to wobble gently in a lifelike way, but to set them all up is time-consuming.

The plastic or rubber full-bodied type does give a more three-dimensional appearance when seen from the side, which is perhaps more realistic than the slim-line shells. However, they are bulkier and a little heavier to carry. There are various makes and types of full-bodied and some do look more like a real woodpigeon than others, so choose the ones which look best.

The paintwork or finish is important. A real pigeon's feathers have a bloom

Shell decoys are light and easy to carry.

or sheen to them but do not shine. Therefore avoid glossy decoys in favour of matt finish. In recent years an excellent innovation has been the flock coating of decoys. This has solved the old problem of shine, whether wet or dry, and they are to be recommended even though they are a little more expensive.

Decoy accessories

Floaters

There are a number of additional decoy rigs which can add visibility to a pattern of static decoys. This becomes an advantage if one is either decoying on a very large field or in a standing crop, such as winter rape, peas or laid crops of corn. This is because static decoys are partly hidden except to pigeons passing directly over them, and it helps to create movement or raise the decoys to attract attention. After all, pigeons arriving at such a field will be looking for movement to draw them to their mates' feeding area.

There are a number of floater cradles on the market which are basically a frame on a length of springy steel rod. A dead bird is mounted on this with wings open and, when set up facing into the wind, it will gently rise and fall in a lifelike way, representing a real bird hovering as it prepares to land. Early in my pigeon shooting days, before such equipment was available, an old gamekeeper showed me an easy way of creating the same effect with hazel sticks cut from the hedgerow. One long one of between three and six feet was cut and pointed at each end. One end was pushed up through the vent of the dead bird to its skull and then the other end was set into the ground supporting the bird at an angle into the wind. A small thin stick about a foot long, with a point on each end, was pushed through the bird's body just below the wing so that each wing was supported in an open hovering position as the pointed ends of the stick pierced the wing joint from underneath. It was simple, cheap and effective. A modern, equally successful DIY floater can be created by using the fibreglass field marker rods which are just flexible enough to do the job, and the cross-piece wing support can be made from a suitable length of wire cut from a wire coat-hanger.

The advantage, however, of the manufactured floater rigs is that they can be telescopic and with fold-away arms, which makes them easier to carry together with your hide poles.

An enterprising development of the floater has been created by Cornishman Chris Green, and can be seen in action on the DVDs he and his

WHAT KIT DO YOU NEED?

son James have produced (www.westcountryfilms.co.uk). They are artificial decoys with wings, mounted on fibreglass rods which swing, tilt and float realistically in the breeze. When used as a group with his wobbling artificials on the ground, they produce an all singing and dancing picture. It is a novel and obviously successful idea to rival the rotary and other electronic decoys.

Cradles

Wire frame cradles are very useful on occasions where the crop is above about six inches tall. The problem then is that decoys set up on the ground are partly hidden except to pigeons passing directly overhead. Crops such as peas or rape, both winter and spring varieties, are vulnerable to pigeon damage at that stage. Therefore cradles which lift the decoys above the standing crop are a big advantage, making them much more visible.

It is possible to make your own but unless you are handy with welding equipment (or have a friend who is) it is easier to purchase ready-made ones.

Wire cradles can lift decoys to make them more visible above a crop.

Flapper

This is a piece of equipment whereby a dead bird is mounted on a cradle which has electric motorised arms to which the outstretched wings are attached. They work off small batteries (1.2 amp, 12v), either acting with nonstop flapping or with a variable timing attachment. This then gives a lifelike flutter interspersed by several seconds pause of variable delay.

Rotaries

Years ago, Archie Coats developed a method of attracting the attentions of a passing bird by holding one wingtip of a dead bird and throwing it out of the hide so that it spun in the air. This worked well, particularly if the hide was near a tree, as it produced the impression of a pigeon dropping from the tree to join the feeding party below. However, it needed a certain skill to select the right moment to throw the dead bird. Too early and the passing bird did not see it, but if too late it would scare it away. However, when the moment of truth was right it did work very well in some situations.

The rotary machine is a modern mechanical version of this technique that, love it or hate it, has been the greatest development of any since decoying pigeons became a sport and a successful method of controlling woodpigeons to protect agricultural crops. It is a device on a stand which is set firmly in the ground. There is a motor, usually the type used for a car windscreen wiper. From the head of this two or even four arms splay out, which are usually about four feet long. On the end of each is a support to hold a dead or artificial bird with open wings. A rotary is powered by any form of 12v battery. It then spins and the birds appear to be flying and turning as they prepare to land. Rotaries are particularly effective on standing crops where static decoys are not easily visible to pigeons coming to the field. They are looking for movement as a clue to where their mates are feeding. The perpetual spinning of the rotary catches the attention of any pigeon from a great distance and it will very often turn to approach.

The original rotary was called the Pigeon Magnet and was developed in 1996 by Phil Beasley, one of the country's most successful pigeon shooting guides. When it was first used it was deadly at attracting pigeons as none had ever seen such a lifelike moving decoy. Actually, soon after I first acquired one I was shooting pigeons on a pick-your-own strawberry field on summer evenings after the customers had gone home. The Pigeon Magnet was very successful and one evening I experimented and tried it where no pigeons would expect to feed – on the car park next to the strawberry field. Sure enough, pigeons flying overhead saw the two spinning decoys and approached within shot. It was not a fluke as I shot over thirty that evening, all landing dead on the car park where people and vehicles had been milling about all day!

Actually, it raised debate as to whether it was ethical to use such a piece of kit which lured pigeons too easily. Some people decided on principle not

WHAT KIT DO YOU NEED?

to use anything but traditional static pattern of decoys, but few refuse to use a rotary today. Interestingly, the pigeons were not slow to wise-up to the rotary and now, because they are seen whirling round in front of most hides, they can be seen as alarm signals to pigeons who have become experienced.

My conclusion now is that certainly young birds, who have not previously seen a rotary, will respond spontaneously, but older experienced birds will often avoid them. The result is that large bags of inexperienced young pigeons will sometimes be shot in August, September and October but in areas that are heavily shot the results are not as good. The approaching leading bird will often come within range but suddenly becomes suspicious and, if not shot at (in the hope that more than one may commit to your decoys), it will veer away, taking any following birds with it. This therefore results in more single birds being shot, with fewer rights-and-lefts. I am convinced that the leading bird, having been fooled into thinking the rotary represented its friends coming in, suddenly believes it to be the opposite and sees it as birds flying away.

The rotary, now manufactured by several companies, is an important piece of equipment but, as suggested, is not effective in every situation. A guide is that if decoys are easily visible, on an open field of drilled corn for instance, then it is not necessary and more opportunities of rights-and-lefts will present themselves without a rotary. However, as stated earlier, it is particularly effective at attracting pigeons when the crop is tall and static decoys cannot be seen easily by pigeons flying over the field. In summary, it

A rotary set-up and all ready to go – note the angle of the birds, tilted inwards.

is a very useful piece of kit, which greatly aids successful crop protection and provides good sport in doing so.

A chicken-and-egg situation relating to the rotary arises if one has not got two dead birds to start with. A development of the rotary solved that by creating artificials which are very light and have special fabric wings which flutter in turn as each bird comes into the wind on its circuit. These are called 'Hypa flap' decoys. Another advantage is that the whole piece of equipment can be very much lighter than one which needs to support the weight of two dead birds. This lightweight rotary is therefore ideal for situations where one has to walk a long way carrying a rucksack full of kit.

There are also other artificial decoys with outstretched wings made to fit on to standard rotary equipment.

Peckers

These are another electrically driven form of decoy. They represent a feeding pigeon as they nod up and down mechanically. They can be set up as a team with a number of wires from one small battery. Personally, I am not convinced that they are a must amongst one's kit. The time they take to set up, weighed against the benefit, makes the latter perhaps doubtful and, by the time you or your dog have tripped over the spider web of wires, a certain irritation is experienced and there are more important aspects of setting up a successful decoy pattern. If you like lots of toys then they will amuse you and the family at Christmas!

Brolly

On showery or wet days it can be useful to build your hide around a brolly. The best type is as used by anglers, which are large and have guy ropes for support. These are commonly made in green, or even camo, but try to find one that is made of strong fabric or it will soon tear if erected near thorn hedges. If used in an open site then you must erect it pointing upwind as otherwise it will be very unstable. Because you will ideally want to shoot birds coming upwind to your decoys this will not be a problem as you will want to sit in the shelter of the downwind side. Unless it is a virtually windless day you cannot set it up above you and so, on virtually all occasions, it will be used on its side. (Many angling brollies have tilt-adjustable poles, or even poles capable of being relocated to the rear, and some have one flat side to aid stability.) Certainly it is worth the trouble not to get wet and cold.

WHAT KIT DO YOU NEED?

Small compartmental travel bag

This is useful for all sorts of small items needed for the day. So let's look in mine to see what I like to have with me:

Contents of travel bag.

1. Sandwiches/packet of crisps and chocolate bar
2. Small flask of coffee and/or cold drink in summer
3. Rope bangers and lighter – if needed to prevent pigeons landing on an adjacent field
4. Clamp clips
5. Transistor radio – good for news, weather and the Test Match
6. Walkie-talkies if there are two of us in separate hides
7. Sticks to set up decoys (½ kebab sticks are ideal)
8. Secateurs
9. Folding saw
10. Small pair of binoculars
11. Handguard if using side-by-side gun
12. Clicker to count birds to be picked up at the end of the day
13. Sunglasses and yellow lens glasses for dull days
14. Hearing protection
15. Recoil pad (can be helpful on a big day, so be prepared – and always optimistic!)
16. Cap
17. Gloves
18. Waterproof leggings
19. Waterproof coat – lightweight for showers
20. Travel bag for small items of kit – mobile phone

It seems a lot of bits and pieces, but actually they fit into a shoulder bag and are important or useful for the success and comfort of what can be a long day.

Additional kit carried in the car

There are a number of items which may or may not be needed, some of which live permanently in the vehicle, others should they be anticipated to be required.

Dog

I'm not sure that my fine golden retriever, Scott, would approve of coming under 'items of kit', or whether he likes to be left in the car. However my pal is indispensable when it comes to picking up at the end of the day. Nevertheless, unless I can sit him back in a wood or in cover at a distance along a hedge, I leave him in the car. Over the years every dog I have had previously, and whose company I have enjoyed in the hide, has gone deaf by the time they were 7 years old. This is sad for them and frustrating for me and so I have adopted the policy of not having a dog in my hide. I miss their company but Scott's predecessor, Conon, the first with whom I adopted this policy, maintained his hearing until late in life, and so far Scott is doing the same. It probably does not matter if you only have the occasional outing but my dogs are like me, lucky enough to get out frequently. I calculated that Conon, who lived to a good age of 15, had been with me to help pick up over 100,000 birds in his life. It is a pity there are not ear muffs for dogs! So, my loyal pal Scottie rests in the car, hoping he may have a busy time at the end of the day. When that time comes he is bursting with energy and does a great job.

If your dog is in the car, it is important to ensure ventilation in the vehicle. Also, in hot weather, put the car in the shade, never in the full sun, and give thought to the fact that the sun will move westward during the day. Obviously, whether he is in the back of your car or in your hide, always have a bowl of water for your dog unless there is another suitable water source available. Working in thick cover on a hot summer evening can be very dehydrating for a dog – and his owner – and standing corn can be particularly exhausting. On such occasions it is a good idea to give a dog frequent rests and drinks. Even five or ten minutes will be sufficient for a dog to regain his drive and energy to work hard again. Nevertheless, be aware of the moment when your dog has had enough, even after frequent rests. I feel it is unkind to over-push his loyalty and I do not want to break his spirit and enthusiasm for next time out.

If picking up in barley it is wise to check your dog's ears every quarter of an hour or so as the awns on the ears of barley have minute barbs as a natural

WHAT KIT DO YOU NEED?

Scott, my pal in action. (Rupert Watts)

way of hitching a lift on passing animals in order to distribute their seed. The problem is that the movement of the dog can cause the barley awns to work their way into the ears. Watch out for this and if your dog is constantly scratching an ear the following day after retrieving in barley, then a visit to your vet may be required.

Whilst on veterinary matters, ensure that your dog has regular tick and flea treatment throughout the summer. Lyme's disease is a serious tick-borne disease for animals and humans and with the increase in the deer population the tick problem is becoming correspondingly greater.

Tools

A *small spade* to level the base of the hide is useful to get your seat on a flat surface. There is nothing worse than a seat which rocks about or is on an uneven angle. It can affect your performance if you are shooting from a sitting position.

A *bow saw* is handy either for cutting branches to make a hedgerow hide or for collecting them to add to the covering of a net hide. A *folding pruning saw* will serve the same purpose.

Loppers are equally good.

I have a short length of thin *rope* about six feet long, with a loop tied on each end. This is used to bind and carry a bundle of cut branches for hide building, or to tow it on the back of the vehicle if building a hide out in a stubble field, for example. (Obviously, do not drive over a crop unless the farmer permits you to drive up the tramlines if the crop is not too tall.)

Sacks for carrying dead birds are essential. Hessian sacks are less easy to acquire these days but the woven plastic type are fine. The key point is that the sack must be of a material that can breathe. Do not collect freshly shot birds in polythene sacks or bags as they will soon overheat and go off. A normal sack will comfortably hold forty pigeons and up to fifty if you are feeling strong. Do not over-fill as there will then be no spare material to make an 'ear' to get a good hold of the top. The most comfortable way to carry a sack full of birds is to lift it across the back of your shoulders so that it can be held by one hand either side of your head. This creates an even weight on your back with least strain. If just carried over one shoulder it becomes uncomfortable because your body is twisted by the weight being on one side. Always put more sacks in the car than you anticipate needing. As with cartridges, be optimistic or you may have a heap of loose birds, feathers and blood in the car.

A *hammer* can be useful for a number of things when setting up. I carry what in Norfolk is locally called a 'lump' hammer, the type with a heavy head and yet short handle that is used by builders chiselling masonry.

Flags are often useful to set up on areas of the field where the pigeons may land rather than coming to your decoys. Sometimes keeping them off other adjacent fields can be important. The flags themselves can be of any type and for many years I have used white polythene fertiliser bags cut open to produce a flag about four feet square. These are tied on to eight-foot canes. I also have larger ones about six feet square for some occasions. However, I have seen people use balloons on canes, or a mass of small flags. The easy way to store and pack flags is to roll them up around the supporting cane or rod.

Sometimes one has to make a hide in a deep ditch. If that is the case I have two strong *eight-foot poles and a lightweight pallet* which I tie on to the top of my vehicle. By putting the poles across the ditch and then the pallet on them, I can make an effective platform well above the water. On this it is then easy to erect a hide which is comfortable and dry.

On winter days, when the wind can be bitterly cold, I take a canvas sheet as a *windbreak* which is fixed to the hide poles on the windward side before the camo nets are draped around. This is a tip worth taking as it is no fun freezing to death while sitting on a field of winter rape in February waiting for pigeons to arrive.

Maybe at times I take things too far, but I have a pair of *body waders* for if I am to shoot with my back to a small river which is too deep for wellies. Scott will happily retrieve across water but sometimes on a flight line there may be a good number of birds that will have dropped well behind me across

WHAT KIT DO YOU NEED?

Large polythene white flags can be very effective at keeping pigeons off areas of a field and steering them to your position.

A multiple of small flags can be effective.

the river. It is not a frequent necessity, but waders can help on such occasions and it is always important to make every effort to pick all the shot birds. Protecting crops is paramount but it is ethical to pick up efficiently and make the most of the good food the dead birds provide, whether for you or for others via your game dealer.

We will talk about *lofting poles* in Chapter 10, but there are occasions, if decoying near a dead tree in summer, or leafless tree in winter, when a lofted decoy can help to catch the eye of passing birds. Therefore, although I seldom take them on a decoying day, I do include lofting poles if I think a bird sitting up a tree would help create a lifelike picture. The regular sets of lofting poles come in bundles of six. However, being six feet long they can only support a decoy about thirty-six feet up the tree. This may be fine for hedgerows, but most trees need a decoy raised double that height and so I have two sets of poles.

Clothing

A short chat about the best clothes needed for pigeon shooting may be of help. Obviously, most of my suggestions are common sense but still some questions arise. Basically wear clothes that are comfortable, suitable for the weather and, above all, of neutral colours. Definitely avoid a white shirt or sun hat in summer; they may be appropriate in every other sport or social context but not pigeon shooting, as any movement will be visibly accentuated and the sharp-eyed woodie will be away before you can get a shot.

You can buy every item of clothing down to underpants in camo colours. However they are not necessary. A mid-tone green or brown jacket (i.e. most shooting jackets) will be fine. As you are to be in a hide ducked down behind a screen of netting and foliage nothing, except perhaps your hat, should be visible to the incoming pigeons. I am not saying that a camo jacket does not help at all, but the advantage over a normal coat as just described will be minimal. It is back to the basic fact that it is *movement* that scares a pigeon, whether in camo or any colour. I have a heavy, warm camo jacket for the winter and this may be an advantage at a time when there is no foliage on the trees and one may be more visible. However in summer a neutral green or brown shirt will be ideal. In the shade of the vegetation you will not be seen.

In some ways I think that the greatest advantage of camo clothing is psychological, in that wearers may shoot with more confidence believing they are less visible. Really, if wearing full camo jacket, hat and trousers, one would not need a hide at all and could stand still with one's back to a hedge.

This does work and would be the case for wearing camo to break up your shape against the background. However, if you are in a hide in normal neutral clothing and keeping still, the pigeons will not see you. The fashion for camo everything is a recent idea that came into vogue around the 1980s to 90s. Prior to that, nobody thought it necessary. Hide discipline to minimise movement is the thing to develop and achieve.

However, whatever colour or choice of *jacket* you wear, the important thing is that it is not too tight, as it must not restrict the swing of your gun. It must be warm in winter but not so bulky that it inhibits smooth and consistent mounting of the gun to your shoulder. It must be waterproof as you will soon get cold if wearing wet clothes for long hours in a hide without much physical movement to keep warm. Large side pockets are useful especially when roost shooting, when I put a box of cartridges into my left pocket and collect my empty cases in my right. However, in a hide I load direct from an open box of cartridges and empties go straight into a bag, so pockets are not so important to me – but maybe you will prefer to load cartridges from a pocket.

Overtrousers in winter can help keep you warm. Whatever the time of year, I always have a thin pair of light waterproof overtrousers rolled up in my bag.

A *hat* of your choice is important as it helps to hide your face. The key thing is that the brim of a hat or peak of a cap should be wide, as it is your face that will be most visible to a pigeon from above. Some pigeon shooters like to wear a *face-mask* to avoid this problem. Personally I find them uncomfortable and unnecessary for decoying; however I do sometimes wear one for roost shooting. This is because the pigeons are arriving at a height above the trees and looking down while you are looking up, and your full face will be very visible at that angle with the result that the birds will jink away on the wind.

Footwear will vary depending on the season and weather. Obviously wellies will be the order of the day on wet days or when the vegetation is wet from rain or dew. Remember, the crop over which you are to shoot may carry a lot of water from rain the previous night, even if the day is fine and dry. On dry days in summer, light canvas boots will be comfortable and suitable.

Gloves can be essential in winter to keep your hands warm. However, they do not need to be a pair, as the one on your trigger finger hand must be either of thin material or be a shooting glove, of which the trigger finger folds back to expose the forefinger. Your other hand, which holds the fore-end of the gun, can have a full glove as bulky as you like, so long as the fore-end can be held firmly.

While talking of keeping warm in winter, there is something of an art in severely cold weather to dressing in a way which maintains body heat but without bulking the upper body so much that it is difficult to mount your gun. It is sensible to wear many thin layers rather than few thick ones. A lesson is learned from mountaineers and those who work or play in arctic conditions. Thermal vests and long johns are ideal, as are the silk form of these. On extreme days I wear both sets, with the silk ones against the skin. Perhaps it is all getting a little too personal to be discussing my choice of undergarments but I am only trying to pass on tips from experience over the years. I know we are preparing for pigeon shooting, but it is a good idea to keep an eye on suppliers of kit for other activities and sports and think laterally as to the advantages of clothing for fishing, skiing, gardening or whatever for our benefit. Having been wet, cold and uncomfortable on many occasions in the past I try to pre-empt this and prepare myself for every eventuality now and in the future – I do not wish to die of hypothermia in a pigeon hide, though when the time comes I would die happy from a heart attack carrying a full sack of pigeons off a field at the end of a good day. A postscript to that morbid thought would be to suggest that, if someone is with me at the time, they should get the pigeons laid out on the garage floor to cool before laying me out, as the game dealer will pay for the pigeons but will give nothing for me!

An inexpensive sport

So now you have an idea of the kit I have to cover every season and situation. The list is extensive but some of it is rarely used. To start with, acquire the basics and the rest will follow. The choice of some items is subjective or personal but worth mentioning as they all have a purpose which helps me and could help you. The story at the beginning of the chapter illustrates that you can start with just a gun and cartridges but not all days are possible like that. However, much of the kit can be improvised or simply made with minimal DIY skills and I have given ideas and options for these. Pigeon shooting does not have to be costly to get started. In fact it is one of the few inexpensive sports these days, as not only can much of the equipment be improvised or home-made, but the sale of pigeons shot can pay for your cartridges if you shoot fairly straight! So you have a sport which you make for yourself, which protects the farmer's crop, costs little or nothing and is a day in the fresh air surrounded by Nature. That cannot be bad for body and soul as you arrive home with good, tasty meat from a wild bird.

CHAPTER 5

PIGEON FEEDING HABITS THROUGH THE YEAR

We will look at the diet of woodpigeons through the year, month by month. However, the bird has a remarkably varied diet and can congregate on unusual crops and produce successful shoots on unlikely fields. Remember, the general licences permit the shooting of woodpigeons at any time of year to protect crops. There are opportunities to shoot pigeons on stubble, fallow ground or other fields when there appears to be no direct threat to a crop. However, those birds may be a threat to crops in adjacent fields the next day. It could be that they have already attacked a crop on the next field and are sitting on ploughed ground or in trees nearby waiting to return later to get another crop-full. Any pigeon on the farm is a threat and shooting is confirmed officially as the best way to control woodpigeons damaging agricultural crops.

It is important to know on what woodpigeons are likely to feed each month because, as you will see from Figure 1 overleaf, 90% of pigeons are shot as a result of decoying. That means shooting them on fields where they are feeding. (These are figures that were deduced by the BASC in 2000 and will vary little over the years.) Roost shooting accounts for only 7% and other shooting for only 3%. These will be birds accounted for when rough shooting or game shooting, when they are not the prime quarry of the day. The low figure of 7% for roost shooting may, perhaps, be surprising as it is such a popular activity after the game season in February and March. However, the fact is that, in reality, the birds shot by this method represent only a very small percentage of the total number of pigeons accounted for in a year. It is interesting to compare Figure 1 with Figure 2, which came from the same BASC survey. The latter represents the percentage frequency of different types of shooting, i.e. the number of shooting days that produced the total number of birds cited in Figure 1. We can see that this backs up the interesting observation that, although roost shooting is so popular, it only accounts for 7% of pigeons shot from 13.3% of shooting days. Conversely, 72.8% of days decoying accounted for 90% of pigeons shot. Therefore decoying can be seen as by far the most effective method of shooting to control woodpigeons. So we are back to the reason why it is important to know on which crops they are likely to be feeding throughout the year.

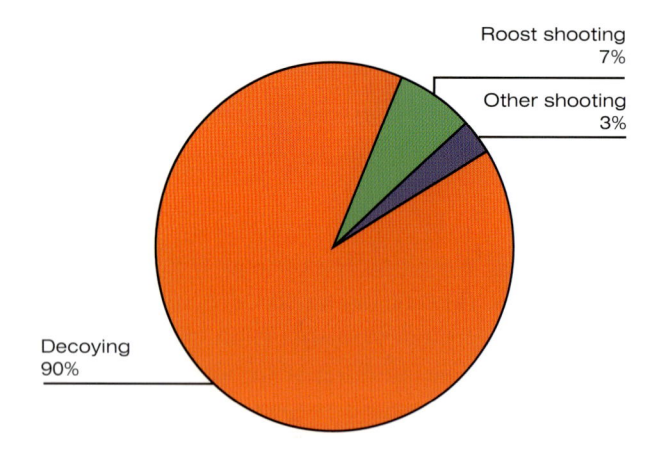

Figure 1. *Proportion of woodpigeons shot by different methods.*

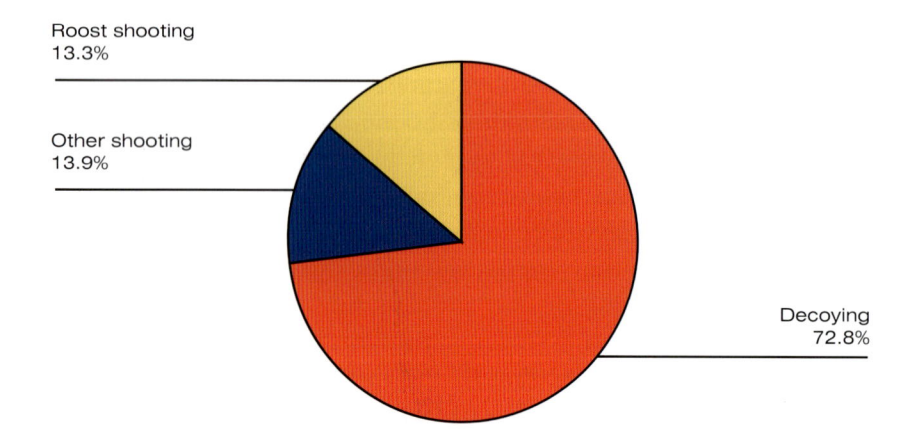

Figure 2. *Percentage frequency of different types of shooting.*

PIGEON FEEDING HABITS THROUGH THE YEAR

Now, if we look at Figure 3, we get more clues as to the fields to be watching. The pie chart represents the percentage of decoying visits made to different crops. To simplify this let us group the arable crops of cereals and pulses (beans and peas) together, e.g. 26.2% + 15.8% respectively, and from this one can see that 42% of visits were decoying on those fields and another 38.1% on oilseed rape. So over 80% of shooting was focused on oilseed rape, cereals and pulses. This figure may be even higher today than in 2000 as the acreage of set-aside, linseed and grass with clover has reduced since then.

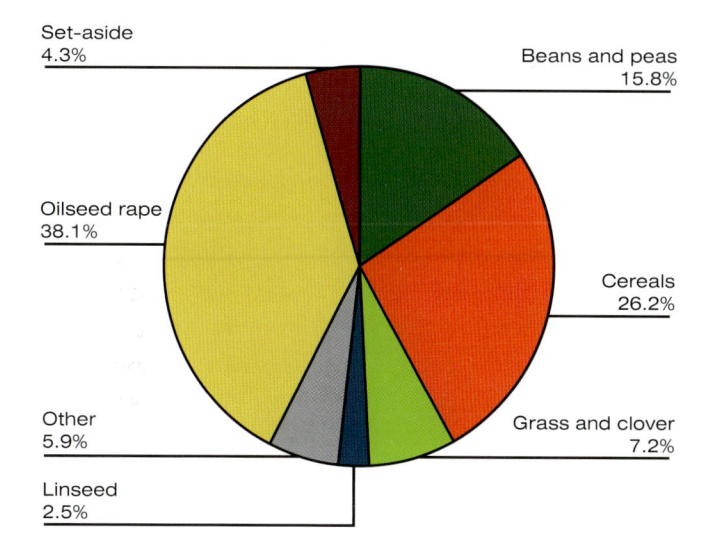

Figure 3. *Percentage of total decoying visits made on different crops.*

The point is that we are led clearly to watch the annual cycle of the farming year as it relates to the three main groups of crop for the majority of our shooting. These are the crops to which pigeons will be causing most damage and where we can focus our attention to best help the farmer to protect them.

So let us look at the food sources for the woodpigeons month by month and how this relates to the way we can shoot them.

WILL'S PIGEON SHOOTING

January

Farmer's Lament, Pigeon Shooter's Joy!

Winter oilseed rape is the crop that will be visited from dawn till dusk of the short days by large flocks of woodpigeons. That sounds exciting, but it is the most difficult and frustrating month in which to shoot good bags of pigeons. This is because the birds are in flocks, a natural protective habit of woodpigeons in winter; which means that even if you are set up to shoot on a field where they are feeding you can only shoot one or two birds out of the many in a flock that may visit your decoys. There could be as many as a couple of hundred in total, but for the odd bird or two you can shoot, the majority will be frightened away by the sound of the shots, probably never to return that day. They will disappear to another field of winter rape. The flock mentality is further encouraged by the constant disturbance of gas guns, farmers patrolling to move flocks on, and shooting. This creates ever-larger flocks from which it is even more difficult to shoot many. This means long hours waiting in cold conditions for frustrating and modest results.

There *are* exceptions when, in a strong wind, the flocks may get split up. Then, if a group of pigeon shooters can cover all the rape fields in the vicinity, the day will be more productive. Things used to be easier when there was not so much oilseed rape grown and fields were isolated; however, with block cropping it is not uncommon now to find areas of several hundred acres in adjoining fields. In some parts of upland Britain, where small mixed farms exist, there are isolated rape fields and it is much easier to protect these as the pigeons are focused on a single crop.

The only good thing about shooting on winter rape is that it is a good way to get your toe in the door to shoot on a farm, as the farmer is pleased

PIGEON FEEDING HABITS THROUGH THE YEAR

to welcome people who help in any way to protect his crop. This might mean long, cold days with little sport but it could lead to you then getting the opportunity to shoot later on the spring drilling, or to protect summer crops when the flocks have broken up and shooting can be more productive.

If the weather is severe, especially if snow is thick enough to cover the oilseed rape, then the pigeons will feed mainly on ivy berries. In the old days, and still in some areas of mixed farming, there may be kale grown for cattle feed, which will then be the main attraction as a food source available above the snow. Brassicas – particularly Brussels sprouts, being tall plants – used to be a major winter food in my part of East Anglia and they are still grown in Bedfordshire. However it is the oilseed rape that is the staple diet for woodpigeons throughout the winter all over the country. It is the crop which has had the most profound effect on the pigeon population as it is so widely grown and a nutritious winter food.

If you are shooting over any crop like kale or Brussels sprouts in snow you will find that pigeons just do not respond to decoys. However, I have found that they will be attracted by movement, so a rotary can sometimes work in these conditions.

A final tip for January, or any winter month when pigeons are feeding exclusively on oilseed rape, is to look for fields where the birds like to collect either before or after visiting rape fields. A field of plough, winter cereals or grass can sometimes become a regular resting place and birds can, at times, be decoyed more successfully there than on the rape itself. It is an indirect way of successfully protecting the crop.

This is the crop content of winter rape of just one pigeon on one day. So multiply this by a flock of a thousand pigeons over four months and it is obvious why shooting is the most important form of crop protection for the farmer.

February

Quite apart from decoying, February is the prime month for roost shooting. The game season is over and so keepers, for whom pheasants have been the priority for the past months, are happy to allow their friends and beaters the opportunity to flight pigeons as they come in to roost. In most areas the birds will be full of rape and their crops will be extended to bursting point with small pieces of the green leaves torn from the foliage of the crop. Others may also be full of ivy berries which are another favourite late winter food. As the main time of shooting is during the last hour of daylight between 4 and 5 p.m. there is a limit to the number of birds that can be shot compared with the all-day event of decoying. Also, the challenge of shooting birds flying high over the trees, whilst being the most exciting and sporting, does not usually result in large bags. However, we will go into more detail about this in Chapter 10.

So, oilseed rape is still the major food source this month, but the big bags will be on chopped maize strips, grown as cover and food for game. In recent years the acreage of game cover has increased enormously as nearly every farm with any game shooting potential now has an organised shoot. Whether this is on a large commercial scale or a modest family or farmer's shoot, most have strips or blocks of maize. This is a great food for game – pheasants in particular – but at the end of the season the tall plants with papery brown leaves may still have uneaten cobs full of the golden yellow seed.

When these maize strips or blocks are chopped or flailed, the remaining cobs are smashed and the seed scattered. Not only do game birds feast on it but rooks and woodpigeons join the party. After a winter of eating green rape this food is a magnet and can produce big bags. This is aided by the fact that, compared with the vast fields of rape, the maize strips are only an acre or two, or even less. This means that any birds are focused and condensed onto small areas, often adjacent to a wood or hedge where it is easy to make a hide. The problem that can arise is that all the strips are chopped at the same time and so, unless there is an organised group to man each strip, the birds will soon find a quiet spot. If you have the ear of the farmer or whoever is involved in the operation, then try to suggest that the strips are cut in rotation so that the pigeons go from one to another over a period of a week or two. This will hold the birds in your area and enable more to be shot. All those accounted for will not then go back to eat more of the farmer's rape, and so the alternative food source will enable a successful method of control and crop protection.

There is also the opportunity in February for weather conditions to allow the lighter land to be cultivated and spring drilling to commence. Land that

PIGEON FEEDING HABITS THROUGH THE YEAR

From time to time it is important to tidy up dead birds which have fallen on their backs.
(Charles Sainsbury-Plaice)

was ploughed in the autumn will have had periods of frost through the winter and, in spring, this dries to create a good seed bed from the frost tilth. Spring beans or tic beans are the first to be drilled. These are like small broad beans and pigeons go mad for them. Some of my best days on spring drilling have been on beans. Sometimes the farmer is so keen to get them drilled that he attempts to drill before the seed bed is ideal and this results in more beans on the surface. The woodpigeons will find these for certain and news travels fast. Pigeons will fly for miles to fill their crops with this nutritious food.

If the ground is fit the first spring barley will also be drilled and this again will be a big draw. It is worth investigating the cropping plan from farmers over whose land you shoot. Ideally you want to be ahead of the pigeons and anticipate the fields that will potentially produce good sport and control the pigeons at the critical time.

It is interesting that shooting on drilled fields, whether in spring or autumn, is more difficult than it used to be. This is because of the development of modern drills that are very efficient at planting the seed consistently at the right depth in the soil and leaving few grains on the surface, except perhaps for some on the headlands where the drill is raised to turn. In the old days the drills were lighter pieces of equipment and, over all but the best seed beds, they bounced along with a percentage of the seed corn being left on the surface. This meant that a number of pigeons would find the field and, over maybe two or three days, a large number would build up. However the problem for the pigeon shooter with the efficient modern drills, which leave so little corn on top, is that a few pigeons can clear the headlands in a matter of hours, preventing a build-up of birds on the field. Therefore, instead of anticipating that all drilled fields may produce a shoot, one now has to look for the ones where there has been a problem, usually of a poor seed bed, to leave enough seed corn to allow a build-up of birds. However, when this happens, shooting over spring drilling can be most exciting. Memories are made of this as, in bright conditions after the winter gloom, birds are seen approaching against a blue sky. The decoys show up so well, a silver blue against the freshly tilled soil, and birds decoy with confidence as they close their wings and stall from a great height, like darts from the heavens.

Other crops to watch in February are lucerne and clover, if they are grown in your area. The tender young shoots are a tasty alternative to the oilseed rape. Also, sometimes, a field of winter wheat that was drilled in the autumn after a crop of potatoes can unexpectedly have a good number of pigeons on it. They are eating the frosted remnants of the potato harvest. The smelly, mushy brown contents of their crops are not very appealing, but the birds love them.

March

Farmers are now into the main spring drilling period – so follow the drill, as do the pigeons. The opportunities and crops are as for February, with rape still the main staple diet. Even when drilled corn is available pigeons will often visit a rape field on the way home to bulk up their crops if not enough grains of seed have been found.

Late chopped maize strips are again to be watched for as not all shoots flail their maize immediately after the game season. I once had an exceptional shoot in April on maize that had not been chopped until then.

The last of the good roost shooting is in March and many birds will have crops full of ivy berries. It is only at roosting time that these birds will be shot as it is not possible to decoy birds when they are feeding on ivy berries which are available on so many trees. Actually I have a theory that there is more ivy on trees and hedges than there used to be and it is because of pigeons. As the woodpigeon population has increased the birds have spread more ivy seeds in their droppings at the base of any trees they sit on by day or roost in at night. These seeds, wrapped in a coating of pigeon guano, will germinate and grow rapidly and within a few years produce more ivy berries to feed more pigeons. The species is cultivating and creating its own food resource.

PIGEON FEEDING HABITS THROUGH THE YEAR

Shooting on spring drilling can produce classic days decoying – note dead birds set up on neck sticks. (Charles Sainsbury-Plaice)

Decoying in March will be most successful between about 11 a.m. until 2–3 p.m. on drilling, but the longer daylight hours will allow birds to feed later and roost shooting will be half an hour later than a month ago.

April

The problem with April and May is that many pigeons will be eating the buds and new leaves of trees. They revert to being truly 'wood' pigeons. Among the comprehensive menu woodland has to offer they particularly love the buds of ash and young leaves of beech as well as flowers of poplar. Pigeons are full of the joys of spring and adults are thinking of breeding. This means more time is spent courting and finding nesting sites, parading, cooing and establishing their own territories around those selected sites, precluding long sorties out to feed on agricultural land. It is not a coincidence that eating tree buds and leaves and establishing territories to breed all happen in the same vicinity in spring. This reduces the number of birds that flight out to feed and therefore decoying is less productive. Those birds that do flight out are, I believe, the young from the later broods of the previous summer and will not themselves breed until mid-summer.

However, April can produce good shoots on drilled fields, especially peas, depending on the weather and where in the country you are located. In the south the drilling may be complete, but in Scotland only just beginning. There

In spring it is a good idea to have a decoy carrion crow set up on one side of the pattern of pigeon decoys.

is at least a month's difference between the same crops in southern England and northern Scotland and whilst my monthly guide is based mainly on southern England do take account of your latitude. To compound the problem the weather one year to the next can alter the picture by as much as a month. A late winter or wet spring will delay drilling wherever, and summer weather will affect harvest accordingly.

The winter flocks of pigeons are now breaking up and this immediately improves prospects for the decoyer, who will get more shots during the day as the birds come in ones and twos or small groups. The daylight hours are lengthening and so the main feeding period will be from about 1 p.m. until 5 or 6 p.m.

Oilseed rape has now taken up the spring nitrogen top dressing and bolted up to seed. The vast acreage of yellow fields brightens the landscape. It is the time when farmers often relax their pigeon deterrents, and gas guns, which have been a regular sound all the winter, now fall silent. However, the pigeons will know of the patches near trees and hedges where the crop was severely attacked in winter and is backward getting away in spring. Often the poor patches then become the focus of ever-greater pigeon damage and although the birds are not in the great numbers of winter they are much easier to decoy. This is for two reasons. First, they are confined to limited areas of a field when the crop is low, and second, the birds are flighting in ones, twos or small parties. I shoot more pigeons on rape at this time of year, with much larger average bags than in the winter when the whole area of

PIGEON FEEDING HABITS THROUGH THE YEAR

In April or May good bags of pigeons can be shot on the backward areas of oilseed rape.

rape is available to marauding flocks. So keep your eyes open for such situations; often the best sport is late in the afternoon between 4 and 6 p.m.

Lucerne, mustard or clover, depending on the farming in your area, can all be successful venues where pigeons are attacking these crops. Years ago weeds in crops were eaten by pigeons. However, with the effective herbicide sprays currently available, one rarely sees crops with a weed problem on the modern farm.

May

This month is similar in most respects to April, both in its problems and its opportunities. However, spring rape can be a crop which is seriously damaged by pigeons. The cornfields, whether drilled in winter or spring, will be green now and of no interest to pigeons, so spring rape or young peas become the focus or their attention. In both cases one or two pecks can

You will please the gamekeeper by killing crows in the spring.

destroy a seedling and seriously reduce the potential yield of the whole crop. This is when the pigeon shooter can really benefit the farmer as, whatever deterrents the latter may use, whether visual scarers or noise from gas guns, those pigeons will eventually get used to them and persist in devouring his crop. However, every pigeon shot is one less to peck the leaves in the weeks and months ahead when the crop is vulnerable. The summer before writing this there was a field of peas in an area with a high pigeon population and I shot the field each week for two months. On occasions I felt I was going out on what I call a 'duty' shoot, since having sole permission to shoot pigeons on this field carried a responsibility to control pigeon damage as effectively as possible. Actually it was successful both as crop protection and for my sport as, in nine weekly outings, I accounted for 800 pigeons. I also shot seventy carrion crows over the period, which collected me brownie points from the keeper. The crop was far more successful than if those pigeons had fed on it every day. So management and co-operation between farmer and pigeon shooter can be of great mutual benefit.

Even in early May do not take your eyes off winter oilseed rape. The low or thin patches may still be attractive to pigeons, some of which may never have deviated onto other crops throughout the spring, but continued to eat the rape which has been their staple diet since last November.

Again, watch for the more unusual crops of mustard, lucerne and linseed. This latter crop is of interest in the early part of its growth from the two-leaf cotyledon stage up to three or four inches tall. I have shot a good bag of pigeons when linseed was first drilled, but the seeds are so small that it seemed amazing that the pigeons would have found any on the surface, let alone considered it worth trying to fill their crops with them.

June

By now all trees are in leaf and more pigeons are coming out from the woods to feed on agricultural crops: both peas and spring rape will be their main attraction. Peas will now be coming on flower and these, together with the delicate young pods, are a favourite food and pigeons can do serious damage to the crop at this stage.

A few years ago set-aside was a required percentage of the land under cultivation. This sometimes had weeds favoured by pigeons, chickweed being a priority. Another favourite was self-set winter barley, which germinated soon after the previous crop was combined and so became the first barley to ripen the following year. This appeared in June, before any other cereal was available. In Norfolk I shot consistently good bags on set-aside in June but now, with new agri-environmental schemes, set-aside is rarely part of the rotation.

Therefore, the first available barley is of the main-crop winter varieties. Years ago there would be areas of barley that would go flat either after a storm or where too much nitrogen had been applied. Today there are far fewer laid areas of barley or wheat; with short-strawed varieties being grown, or the application of growth retardants which prevent straw growing to its normal height, the corn crops stand well. However, sometimes in the area where the fertiliser spreader turns on the headland of the fields it creates an overlap. This double dose of nitrogen will produce taller, weaker stalk growth, which cannot support the weight of the ear. This can then lead to a strip of laid corn conveniently about ten yards out from a hedge. The pigeons find this at the milky stage before the seed hardens and it is a most attractive and nutritious food. A good shoot can be had on these areas where pigeons can do considerable damage by totally stripping the laid corn of every ripening grain.

As laid patches are now uncommon the pigeons have a new strategy and have taken to landing in the tramlines. These are the wheelings of the tractors when spraying or top dressing a crop throughout the period of its growth. It is difficult to shoot pigeons when they are feeding like this as they can land anywhere in the tramlines covering the whole field. This, combined with the difficulty of showing decoys and picking up any shot birds in the standing corn, makes effective crop protection difficult. A rotary can solve the first problem as it shows two spinning decoys above the crop, but even with a good dog picking up is difficult without creating more damage to the crop. This creates a dilemma as it is unethical to shoot without making the best attempt to pick the shot birds, but retrieval is unacceptable if the crop damage is disproportionate to the birds shot.

Every situation is different and so a personal decision needs to be made in conjunction with the farmer. If dogs can work without damaging a crop and a big bag is anticipated, I organise help from the keeper or picker-up friends who are keen to have work for their dogs at that time of year. They arrive in the evening at a pre-arranged time and as a team we set about the job. I recall a time in Norfolk when, at the end of a very busy day, there were 469 birds counted down on my clicker in the laid barley. With eleven dogs we worked through the cool of the evening with frequent rests for the dogs, when we let them drink from the stream nearby. Before the day started I had put cans of beer to cool in the water for those kindly helping. With that team we accounted for 90% of those dead birds hidden in the standing crop. It would never have been possible for me alone with my one dog to have been that effective. More importantly it would have been unethical to shoot that many pigeons, even though protecting a crop being seriously damaged, without making arrangements for help with picking up.

If you are fortunate enough to shoot over farms where vining peas are grown, these are harvested in June or July and the stubbles can be a great attraction for pigeons, when good bags can be achieved.

July

So, having moved from winter-drilled barley to wheat, both mainly preferred by pigeons at the milky stage, the next big attraction is the winter oilseed rape. This crop needs a low moisture content before it can be combined and the farmer has three options to prepare it for harvesting. First, it can be cut in rows and left to dry, a process called 'swathing'. Second, the crop can be sprayed to kill the plant and so stimulate desiccation, causing early ripening of the seed, and third, the rape can be left to mature naturally and the seed ripen. As the first two methods create an earlier possibility of combining they are sometimes used to stagger the harvesting period by swathing or spraying off some fields while leaving others to ripen naturally later.

Pigeons absolutely love rape seed. Small though it is – little larger than a pinhead – they find it and will work long enough on a field to fill their crops. They can appear to get hooked on this seed. Whether it contains any drug-like substance or is just so tasty to the woodpigeons I do not know, but they certainly travel a distance for it when it is available. The birds will attack it when in the swathe as it is easy to perch on the rows. Some farmers will welcome you to shoot at that stage but, as the seed pods become very brittle, any shake or disturbance to them can cause the seeds to shed and so be lost. Therefore check whether or not a farmer will permit you to shoot the swathed crop. Otherwise, although you will be protecting it from pigeon damage, you may be causing more damage yourself.

However, when combined, the stubble is certainly shootable, and if allowed to stand for a few days before being cultivated it can attract large numbers of pigeons. Some farmers send in the cultivator and discs immediately; others allow the spilled seed to germinate and then plough it in. This creates a benefit to the following crop, usually winter wheat, by having little problem with volunteer rape and the soil is improved by the green manure that's incorporated.

George Digweed's official record bag of pigeons – 661 shot in a day – was achieved on oilseed rape stubble. On a long summer's day birds will steadily visit a field to feed, weather permitting, so big bags can be expected. They may not actually be doing damage on that stubble but, whilst the opportunity is there to control a good number, those shot will not ravage the oilseed rape of the following winter at a time when it is so much more difficult to achieve the same effective control.

Two problems have arisen in many areas of large-scale rape production. First, as has been mentioned earlier, the system of block farming makes it difficult to cover a number of fields which may total hundreds of acres, and this applies at any stage of the crop. Second, most farmers are keen to cultivate the stubble close on the heels of the combine and so there is no time for pigeons to congregate on a field, let alone provide a day's shooting. There can, of course, be an advantage in that if any fields are not cultivated immediately the birds, with little chance of going elsewhere, will concentrate there and can produce a good shoot.

So rape is a key crop in modern farming and the pigeon shooters' life throughout the year. It supports an ever-growing population of woodpigeons throughout the winter which, prior to the 1970s, would suffer considerable natural losses at that time of year. Rape produces the opportunity for many pigeon shooters to go out on many days throughout the winter to control pigeons where they are doing most damage to the crop, though this can be a frustrating and cold exercise. However, the stubble can be the summer bonus when good bags are made by those who have helped protect the farmer's crop in winter.

In the middle of summer pigeons often do not flight out to feed until the evening, especially in hot weather. The best shooting will normally be from 5 p.m. onward. Therefore bear this in mind when doing your reconnaissance and try to spy the field at the time when most activity is expected.

August

This month will again be focused on rape stubbles where they have not been ploughed or cultivated, though the timing may depend on where you live. In northern England and Scotland this will be the main month of rape harvest.

In July we looked for rape stubbles that were allowed to green up before being cultivated, but it isn't just agricultural practice that can lead to the stubble being left to lie for a while. With the advent of biofuels for power stations, the rape straw has a market and some farmers will therefore wait and bale the coarse rape straw after it has dried sufficiently. Unlike cereal straw which is fit to bale at the time of harvest, the rape straw is still green and needs several days of dry weather before baling. This is a window when the pigeons can find and build up on rape stubble.

In my part of East Anglia, where large areas of rape are block farmed, it can be a problem to cover the area and so, rather like in winter, it can pay to get a few pals to co-ordinate a day to cover the area. Just prior to writing this, three of us arranged to shoot a big block of 250 acres. This was rolling ground with three woods between the vast fields. These woods had just been stocked with young pheasant poults and so the edges were out of bounds. However, by erecting three hides and strategically placing nineteen large white flags, three rope bangers and our three vehicles to keep birds off some areas and steer them to the vicinity of our decoys, we kept the birds on the move and ended the day with over 300 pigeons in the bag. So co-operation and planning can help solve difficult situations.

In August the wheat harvest is fully underway and this opens up vast acres of stubble available for pigeons. It is a very busy time for the farmers, who will vary the time of stubble cultivation according to the staff available. Certainly those

Wheat stubbles offer either spilt grains or, as in this case, whole ears of corn. (Don Brunt)

fields that are to go into winter oilseed rape will either be prepared for drilling or be direct-drilled. The latter will, in effect, just create a slot for the seed and leave the stubble.

Peas will be harvested and though the pigeons usually do not feed on pea fields when the ripening pods are tough and foliage becomes dry, as soon as they go through the combine the pea stubble can be a great draw. Once again the problem is that the farmer is keen to cultivate the ground in preparation for the following crop, usually winter wheat. However don't miss the opportunity of a shoot on pea stubble if it arises.

September

This is the month when pigeons have the greatest opportunity to feed on stubbles of various crops. With so many available it can be difficult to find a field of preference. However, September and October are the months when there are the greatest number of young birds on the wing and being inexperienced these will decoy well. The young birds with more brown plumage and no white neck ring will make up a large percentage of the bag at this time of year. At home we love to eat roast young pigeon and it is an opportunity to select the largest, fattest birds and prepare them for the freezer. We stock up for the year and so enjoy eating the tender and tasty young birds in every month.

Beans are the last of the crops to be combined, both winter and spring varieties. The stubbles can be a magnet to pigeons, but often not until October when the hard beans lying on the ground have been softened up by rain. The problem again is that, as beans are a break crop, the stubbles are soon ploughed up to prepare a seed bed for the winter wheat which follows. Although farming units are now larger, the stubbles disappear faster, owing to the power of modern tractors and scale of cultivation equipment which can rip up a hundred acres a day. Everything happens so fast that bean stubbles in October are becoming a thing of the past in my part of the country. I used to try to spend my birthday on 9 October decoying somewhere on a bean stubble as it was such a joy, but have not had that opportunity for several years now.

It is interesting as I consider the farming year from the pigeon's point of view and that it is a constantly changing and evolving pattern. Over my lifetime there has been a total revolution from small mixed farms to large scale agribusinesses. Most farms of my youth in the 1950s were modest in scale and family run, as is still the case further west and in the north, where smaller fields and grass for stock still exist because of the hilly topography and high rainfall. However, here in eastern and much of central England there are fewer and fewer farmers cultivating larger and larger acreages with massive 400–500 horsepower tractors. These economies of scale are possible on the large fields of flat or rolling land. So, in the eastern half of Britain, there has been an agriculture revolution for cereal farming and, as I have pointed out earlier, the growing of oilseed rape has actually enabled the pigeon population to increase dramatically as winter losses are no longer the controlling factor.

Such crops as vining peas (grown for freezing), spring rape and hemp are all new crops never seen until recent times. I am nostalgic perhaps about the past and the fun it was as a child to play on a farm, but the demand for food and the world market forces have stimulated the changes and development of modern farming which produce so much more food per acre. This has been possible with selective plant breeding and yield improvements and sprays to control weeds, diseases and insects, which are effective but at times controversial. Genetically modified crops (GMs), are not permitted yet in the UK but are waiting in the wings and, as world pressure increases further to demand more food, the GMs will be permitted sooner or later. At least the delay will allow further research and improvements. Hopefully that will ensure the genes that are modified do not come back to bite us and lead to more problems than they solve. However I remain positive and optimistic that this could be possible.

Quite why I seem to digress into discussing agricultural changes when talking about pigeons in September I am not sure, but perhaps the season when the harvest is gathered in was an appropriate moment to think about the subject and the future.

October

This is the month that sees fast-moving changes to the landscape. Stubbles disappear and field after field is drilled with winter cereals. By the end of October about 80% of arable land will be drilled and another large acreage will be added as sugar beet is lifted. This means that pigeons have an enormous choice of food. So watch for a poorly drilled field where the seed has not gone in as well as the farmer may have intended; here there will be a window of a day or two to get a bag of pigeons before they move on. However, if you still have a bean stubble in your area this will be a draw for pigeons, whatever other food is available. Sometimes, even when a bean stubble has been cultivated and drilled, there will be beans on the surface, especially if only shallow cultivation was carried out prior to drilling, and there is a move to this in recent years rather than ploughing bean stubble as was usually done in the past.

The year before writing this, the 150-acre field behind my house was shallow cultivated and drilled with winter wheat after beans had been harvested. Many beans were still on the surface and after a week or two the wheat had germinated, the field was a haze of pale green and a good number of pigeons had found it. Two of us shot from either end of the large field and picked up 380 – a good day indeed, but ten days later the birds were back and with another friend we shot over 700 in a gale. In the wind the pigeons could not locate the shots and just kept coming – at the peak of sport I shot a hundred in forty-five minutes, which was certainly my fastest century.

November

Late drilling should be watched as the last fields will often hold pigeons longer when there are no new fields on which to feed.

Oilseed rape that was drilled in August and September is not usually of interest to pigeons while so much corn is available on stubbles or drillings. However, in the last week or two of November pigeons will start on the rape and good bags can be achieved before the farmer becomes over-concerned and sets out his gas guns and scarers.

At this time of year tree seeds, particularly acorns and beech mast, can draw birds into the woods to feed. It is difficult to make good bags of pigeons if this is the case, but flight lines along favoured belts or the edges of woods can provide sport in areas where the keeper is not trying to hold his pheasants. In years of a really heavy acorn crop the pigeons can disappear into the woods for months. I remember one winter when pigeon shooters were seriously worried as no pigeons could be found on rape in their area. Of course the farmers were delighted, but the answer was that the woodpigeon was back in its favourite habitat thriving on Nature's bounty.

December

Now we have come the full circle and unless it is a good acorn year the birds will be flighting out at dawn from their roosting woods to feed on rape. These flocks are now augmented by migrant birds from northern England and Scotland as well as from northern Europe. With short daylight hours the birds spend much of their day feeding. As the green crop is digested quite quickly the pigeons will feed then sit back in trees or woodland before taking another feed. This may happen on and off all day, but the late afternoon feed will be the serious one when they fill their crops to bursting point to fuel them through the night. It is the start of the frustrating time of chasing large flocks around many fields of oilseed rape and it is not easy to make a good bag.

Recap

Keep your eyes open throughout the year – and not only on the obvious crops, as unexpected things can happen. Here are some examples of this which I have used to my advantage and produced good bags.

One year in late June a field of wheat grown as trial crops suddenly had strips cut to separate the different blocks. The milky wheat was at a perfect stage to attract pigeons and so, when laid flat on the ground in the strips, it was soon buzzing with birds. With decoys set up on the outer edge a bag of 263 was shot in an afternoon. Sadly that policy was never used again and the wheat was either drilled or the inter-rows were rotovated soon after the young crop emerged.

It is illegal to bait a field for pigeons but one February a farmer friend was clearing out a barn and there were a few hundredweights of beans which he decided to put into a fertiliser applicator and spread on a patch of rough ground to get rid of them. Well, every pigeon in the area came off his rape and fed on this bonus feast – again a shoot of over 200.

A third example was on land destined for development and the road network was being built. The last crop on the fields was wheat and the following year the land was abandoned for farming, but the spilt corn from that previous harvest had grown and there was a surprising crop in spite of weeds. At the end of the summer some was even combined, but the rest was mown. This left a carpet of cut weeds and grain from the volunteer wheat. The pigeons loved it and after negotiations with the contractors I had permission to shoot. I had one or two good days even though bulldozers and earthmoving trucks and lorries were passing by within range. Obviously I was only able to take shots at safe angles, but the pigeons had no fear of the contractors' plant machinery.

These are three examples of pigeons being opportunists when a surprising food source became available, so always keep an eye open for the unexpected situations, as they may make the best day's shooting. Whether these are directly or indirectly protecting crops, a dead pigeon will not come back another day to damage a crop on adjacent fields.

CHAPTER 6
PIGEON SHOOTING OPPORTUNITIES

Go with a friend

Probably most people's first experience of pigeon shooting, whether it be decoying or roost shooting, will be going out with a friend. This first experience will be formative in inspiring you to enjoy the challenge of outwitting a truly wild bird in its environment and the testing shots it can produce at every angle, height and speed. Equally, it may not appeal to spend hours in all weathers waiting for birds that sometimes never arrive. The woodpigeon is a quarry which, despite one's years of experience will still produce surprises, both good and bad. Pigeon shooting is not a sport for the impatient, but it can be addictive and you will find you cannot wait for the next opportunity to get out to pit your wits against this bird and for the satisfaction of enjoying a few memorable shots.

Unless you continue to go regularly with a friend, pigeon shooting is rather a sport for the loner. Therefore if you need a sport which is more sociable (and with a known expectation of a certain amount of shooting) then perhaps clay shooting would more appropriate. However, many people enjoy both – I do occasionally enjoy shooting clays with the purpose of experimenting or practising shots which I may experience in the field.

A day out with a guide

There are a number of individuals and organisations set up to take people out decoying for a day. At the time of writing, this costs in the region of £100 to £150, depending on the area of the country. Sometimes the charge may

Pigeon Country

also vary depending on the success or failure of the day – which is sensible for a quarry that can be elusive or prolific. Personally, if I were a guide (which I am not), I would ask a modest fixed fee for any day but then charge for the shots fired on top of that. This would be fair and people would then pay in a way that was directly proportional to the sport enjoyed.

The advantage of going with a guide is that he will produce all the kit required, so you just turn up suitably clothed, with your gun and cartridges. Importantly, he will (or should have) done the reconnaissance the day before you shoot. He may have several clients out but, unless it is an organisation with a number of people involved and shooting over a large area, it is not easy to produce consistently good shooting. Most guides are reputable but some may try to over-egg it by taking more clients than they know they can offer the opportunity of much shooting. However, a successful guide soon gets a good reputation so, ideally, follow a recommendation.

PIGEON SHOOTING OPPORTUNITIES

The plus side is that you just arrive on the day and your guide will have arranged kit and venue for your shoot. This is useful for the person who is heavily committed to a busy business life or has limited time. The downside is that there is a great deal of pleasure in carrying out your own reconnaissance and arranging a day accordingly – then the shoot is all the more satisfying. Half the pleasure for me is in the reconnaissance and planning the day in discussion with the farmer. However, I am fortunate that in my day-to-day life I can arrange time to keep an eye on the farms over which I shoot and can anticipate where I will find pigeons throughout the year.

If you are limited for time and want to find a guide within a sensible travelling distance, select someone recommended or known by your local gun shop. Often there are advertisements in the shooting press, but ask a few questions when you contact them such as how they charge, what bags individuals have been shooting recently and what is the average bag or number of shots you can expect. Check that the bag figures are not derived from the total a group of clients shot in a day. It may sound good if you hear the average day produces a hundred pigeons, but not if it is the total from four or more guns. Of course it can work both ways, as it is very frustrating for guides to take out people who fire a lot of shots without producing pigeons in the bag!

I know one guide, a colourful character in Hertfordshire, who is now retired. He took a particular client out on several occasions; the man's performance was not impressive and he was having a lot of shooting to achieve bags of twenty or thirty. The client said it would be nice to be taken to a field where he could shoot a hundred pigeons. The guide replied rather curtly that as long as the chap had a hole in a certain part of his anatomy he would never shoot a hundred pigeons! Surprise, surprise – the client never came again.

What tends to happen is that good guides build up a client list of Guns who can shoot reasonably well. They charge a fair price and the clients have good days on average. Then all parties are happy and, compared with game shooting, the cost is very reasonable when you consider that the average driven brace of grouse costs more than £150 or a driven pheasant £30 to £40.

Pigeon shooting clubs

Some areas of Britain have organised clubs and they run a crop protection service free to farmers. It is worth visiting the BASC GoShooting website which carries contact details of affiliated clubs. There are positives and negatives to woodpigeon shooting clubs. The positives are that the organisation of farms, permissions and opportunities day-by-day are co-ordinated by the club and there will be the social side of meetings and gatherings. The negative element can be that farmers phone for help frequently – perhaps on winter oilseed rape where to shoot a bag is very difficult, but they want a Gun there to bang about and act as a scarecrow. This can be a misuse of the club's facility but I'm sure the benefits probably outweigh the disadvantages and it is a way of getting started and gaining experience.

Getting permission

Going shooting with a friend or a guide relies on their having permission to shoot on the farms involved. However, sooner or later, you will want to arrange shooting on farms for yourself. Obviously this is easier if you live in the country, or at least have contacts from where to start. It is not as easy now as it was when I started because there are many more people interested in pigeon shooting than in the 1960s. Also, I live in the country and the family who farm the area around the village have been part of the community in which I grew up. Therefore I was always welcome to shoot pigeons on their land. There were seldom many pigeons on their crops but a field or two of spring barley drilling or stubbles in autumn made an outing in my formative years. I was learning and had limited means of transport and so if I could not walk or bicycle to a field I was stuck.

Then, in my early twenties, I found a way to meet my hero of pigeon shooting, the late Major Archie Coats. By then I was an art student in London with a small car and so could slip off down to Hampshire from time to time. Archie and his wife, Prue, were so kind and generous to me over many years, and days out with Archie were always an adventure. We chugged along country lanes in his battered blue Land Rover with the back full of a jumble of nets, poles, guns, cartridges and sacks of dead birds for decoys. Every field we passed had a story. It was like turning the pages of a boy's annual with an exciting tale of pigeons shot in wind, rain, snow or a gale from a relevant hedgerow or tree in which Archie had manned a hide and shot a prodigious bag. From his pipe, held between his teeth at the side of his mouth, blue smoke billowed between sentences.

On those days with Archie I learned so much as he taught me how to set out decoys with heads held up on twigs from the hedgerow. Hide building was simply a camouflaged old army tank net on metal stakes. As mentioned earlier, I sat uncomfortably on an upturned oil drum, perhaps with a sorbo rubber cushion, sometimes in a bale hide which was a favourite of his. In those days all bales were the small type, not the jumbo round or square half-ton jobs of today. Pigeons decoyed well and my memory, of course, recalls only the good days and tends to obliterate others when the birds either could not be found or, having been found, did not return. However Archie was a master of the job and had such confidence that things would work, to the point that if they did not it was not his fault, but that of the pigeons!

Everything seemed somehow so easy and I absorbed it all without fully acknowledging him for teaching me so much.

I know I have drifted off the subject of getting permission but it is part of my story because, as I became more experienced, my bags of pigeons increased and I began to seek permission from other farmers in my area. The secret, I found, was to expand by the ripple effect – I would approach a farmer I did not know saying that I shot pigeons on Mr So-and-So's farm next door. Farmers are naturally wary of allowing people they do not know onto their land, but if there is a direct or indirect reference from their neighbour then usually the door is opened and one is welcome.

In addition to that strategy, I never went to ask permission until I saw a potential hundred bird day. Then, having got tentative permission, I could return that evening to tell the farmer of my success. That cemented his confidence in me and from then on he would often telephone me when he had pigeons. Also he would tell his neighbours with pride of the young chap from the next village who shot a hundred pigeons on his field. So I soon built up an area over a good number of farms.

Now I was fortunate, but I tell that story to illustrate how you can develop an area and this is still the best way today. The difficulty now is that with many people interested in shooting pigeons most farmers have already got one or two (or more) regular pigeon shots. However, do not let this put you off as there are openings still available and a number of questions arise. Are those who shoot on a farm available always when needed to protect a crop? How successful are they? Is there an opportunity to get a toe in the proverbial door by volunteering to keep pigeons off rape in winter? Often others may not turn up when needed, and if you are prepared to come regularly, even if the shooting is poor, it could mean that you are welcome on the better crops of spring drilling and stubbles later.

Much more land is now managed for game shooting and in such cases a gamekeeper will be an integral member of the team. It may be that the pigeon shooting is a perk for his regular beaters; if so you might offer your help in that way to gain the opportunity to shoot pigeons on the farm or estate.

WILL'S PIGEON SHOOTING

This good number of pigeons shot on autumn drilling will never eat any rape in the winter on adjacent fields.

The key is that you must earn the trust of farmer, keeper, farm manager or whoever controls the pigeon shooting on the farm. To do so you must follow basic rules such as:

1. Always phone to notify those concerned on days you are to shoot.
2. Always check that you will not be in the way of any agricultural activity that day.
3. Always leave gates as you find them – if in doubt, close them.
4. Always leave your hide tidy, having taken away all rubbish and empty cartridge cases.
5. For hide building do not cut and damage any young trees and only select species like elder, sycamore, thorn or willow, not oak, beech or hornbeam for instance.
6. Always acknowledge everyone you meet on the farm, even if it is only a wave to a tractor driver in his cab.
7. Always be polite to anyone walking about, even if you believe they

PIGEON SHOOTING OPPORTUNITIES

should not be there. You may find they are friends of the farmer, or even his family. It's not good news for you if they arrive home saying they have been sworn at by a man hiding in a hedge wearing camo.

8. Following on from the last point, do not jump out from a hide in a hedge at the last minute if anybody walks past, as they may well have a right to be there and they should not be frightened. It's better to walk out slowly into the open well before they approach, take off your ear muffs and headgear so they can see your face, and say 'Hello' with a smile.
9. Always carry your shotgun certificate, or at least a copy, in case you are approached by police.
10. All who shoot must have public liability insurance. This is included automatically with membership of the BASC, Countryside Alliance or NGO. It is a good idea to carry your membership card with you.
11. It can be wise to take a spare gun, in which case it is recommended that it should be hidden in your locked car and, as an added security precaution, the fore-end should be removed and kept with you.
12. Remember at all times you are an ambassador for all who shoot. Therefore be polite and friendly, do not create conflict. Farmers do not want hassle; they want harmony among all those on their land.
13. Remember you are there with the farmer's permission to do a job and protect his crop. It may be your sport, but his crops are his livelihood.

So, there are a number of ways of obtaining pigeon shooting and, from my experience, I can assure you that if you are passionately enthusiastic people will notice and doors will open with opportunities.

As you build up contacts with farmers, farm managers or gamekeepers it is a good idea to keep their telephone numbers readily available either on your mobile phone or in the back of your diary as I do. Often one needs to contact somebody while out on reconnaissance, or even when in the hide should a question arise or something occur which the farmer should know about. Communication by all involved is very important to avoid any misunderstanding.

CHAPTER 7
HOW TO SHOOT PIGEONS

There have been a number of good books written about pigeon shooting and many have covered every aspect except the actual use of the gun to do so.

Before going pigeon shooting or, for that matter, shooting any live game, it is important to achieve a good degree of proficiency. This is not only a responsible and ethical approach to shooting live quarry, but also develops your confidence in doing so. Therefore, visit a shooting ground and make use of the excellent instructors who work there. A good instructor will make the safety element clear at all stages of gun handling. He will check your gun for fit and your eyes for dominance to ensure that, when mounted, your master eye is aligned along the barrel. Also that, with your cheek comfortably on the stock, your master eye is positioned just above the rib. If it is too high you will see a lot of the rib and the gun will shoot high, but if too low the rib will be hidden and the gun will shoot low.

Shooting instructors will have their own ways of introducing beginners to shooting competently and safely. For the more experienced shot there are two clay disciplines which will be helpful for pigeon shooting. The skeet range is useful because the targets come at all angles and a low trajectory, and most decoyed pigeons will offer shots of that sort. Pigeons will be, on the whole, much slower than skeet but if you can learn to shoot skeet targets consistently you will be easily able to adapt to the slower bird. Mind you, a downwind crossing pigeon can be every bit as fast as skeet and therefore you will be familiar with all those targets.

The second discipline is of a 'sporting' layout. These can be targets of all heights, angles and speeds. That may seem odd or unnecessary, but the woodpigeon will produce shots represented by nearly every target experienced, with the exception maybe of 'springing teal'. Even the 'rabbit' crossing or quartering is like a low pigeon just above the ground. The 'battue' which curls and twists in the air is a target for which, like a pigeon, one has to select the moment when it can be shot successfully.

For the experienced shot there are shooting grounds where you can just arrive and collect a counter which plugs into a socket at each stand and records the number of clays used. This is great fun with a friend or two, but can be enjoyed alone as you can select a 'delay' button on each panel prior to pressing to call the bird. This then comes after about five seconds, in which time you have prepared for the shot. This form of clay practice can therefore be successful with or without an instructor, though obviously an instructor would need to be booked in advance. However, just to turn up and pay for clays used is very reasonably priced – at the time of writing, between 20-25p per clay. So good practice, and a fun couple of hours of say a hundred targets, will cost £20-25. You can either use your own cartridges or buy them as you check in. I thoroughly recommend this form of practice.

To take things a stage nearer reality, you can use a shooting seat and practise all the shots from a sitting position, as if you were in a hide. The key to shooting from a seated position is to face nearly 45° to the right of front (assuming you are a right-handed shot) – see Figure 4. This actually replicates the angle of your hips when standing correctly to shoot. If you sit with your feet central to the front you will severely limit your swing to the right as you will run out of movement as you twist round. This will either prevent you taking the shot or result in shooting low as the right shoulder drops and the gun follows below the line of the bird. So practise shots at all angles, having prepared yourself to be sitting at the comfortable angle to address the bird (see Figure 5 overleaf). With practice this is not difficult and becomes natural. I use a swivel seat as described earlier, which is comfortable and permits easy movement to either side.

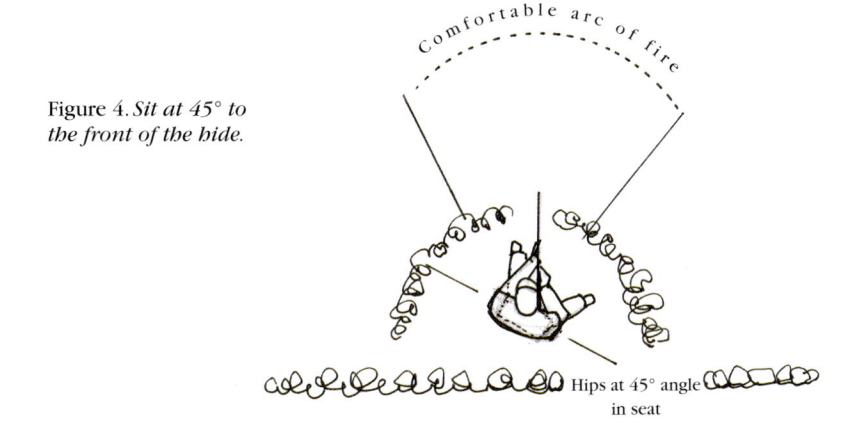

Figure 4. *Sit at 45° to the front of the hide.*

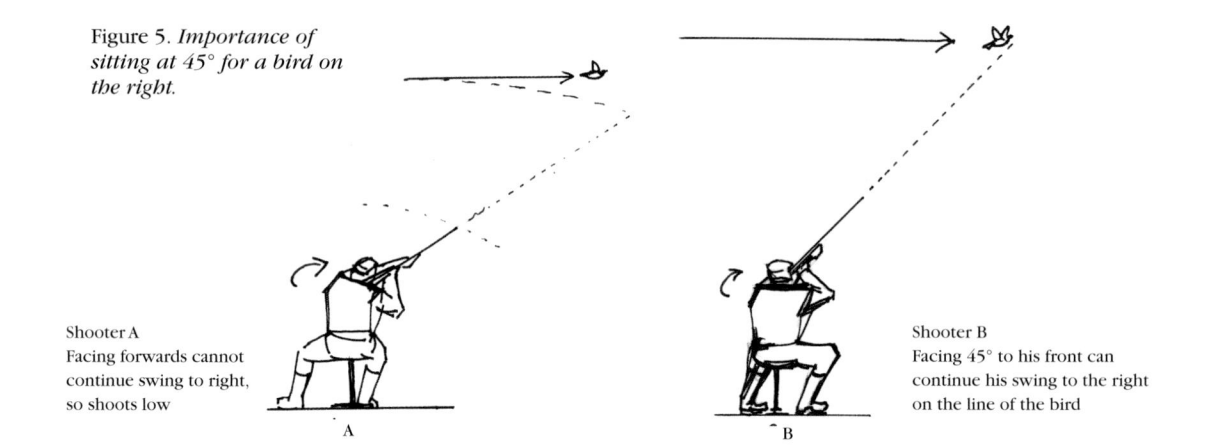

Figure 5. *Importance of sitting at 45° for a bird on the right.*

Shooter A
Facing forwards cannot continue swing to right, so shoots low

Shooter B
Facing 45° to his front can continue his swing to the right on the line of the bird

You may say, 'Well I'll just practise on the pigeons', but as each one will arrive presenting a different shot it is difficult to learn. It is much better to practise on clays that can produce the same target time after time and enable you to read the line, height and speed to perfect each shot. This will not only bring more accuracy, success and confidence when in the field but is more ethical in that each bird will be killed cleanly. Live quarry is not just there for practice.

So, now let us apply these skills, competence and confidence to the real thing. Again remember *the paramount thing above all else is safety*. A shotgun is a lethal weapon and if an accident can happen at some time, for someone, it will. Occasionally one reads of a tragedy of somebody killed when pigeon shooting – normally when two people are sharing a hide – but even on one's own there is a risk. Never assume it cannot happen to you; always be aware of every aspect of safety – all the time.

Let us assume you are alone in a hide. Removing your gun from its sleeve is the last thing you do after building a hide and setting out decoys. Make sure you have space, whether you are to shoot sitting or standing. Open your gun before removing it fully from the slip and, before you load, look through the barrels to check that there are no obstructions. With the barrels pointing at the ground in front of you, load the gun and close it by raising the stock to the barrels still held in the loading position. Do not close the gun by lifting the barrels to the stock as, should it go off, it will be pointing up at head level should someone previously unseen appear.

If your gun closes with the safety catch automatically engaged, fine; if not, ensure that the manual safety is 'on'.

To hold the gun in the hide, if sitting, rest the butt on the ground with barrels pointing up and forward. Personally, being right-handed, I have my gun held beside my right knee angled as suggested. Alternatively it can be on your lap pointing down. This is assuming that, if you have a dog, it is sitting or lying behind, not in front of you, on the ground. The dog must be safe at all times with the barrels never pointing in its direction.

In theory a gun can only fire when the trigger is pulled, but mechanical failures do occur and one must always assume that, if a gun is loaded, it could fire. Therefore it must, at all times, be pointing away from danger. A safety catch may not be on and a trigger can be engaged by anything from a twig to a coat cuff. *So please never take safety for granted.*

If two of you are to shoot together then the safety element becomes so much more important, as the danger of an accident is obviously increased enormously. There are a number of ways to minimise this:

1. It is safest – and strongly recommended – for only one person to shoot at a time while the other has his gun in its slip. The second person is then a 'spotter' for approaching birds and usually the two will swap over after so many shots have been fired. This is fairer than a time factor or number of pigeons shot unless both shoot as well or as badly as each other!
2. The same as above, but the non-shooter just has his gun unloaded.
3. If both are to shoot together as a team then I am sure the safest way is to have, in effect, two single hides built next to each other. This ensures a partition which, though not shot-proof, is preventing a gun being swung sideways in the hide: a positive barrier of a hide pole, which must be tall enough to stop either Gun swinging across the front of the other. (This also helps prevent birds coming from either side being able to look down on the further shooter, who may be visible.)

The main safety element is that each person is limited to shooting to their front or respective side. This is the only way I will ever shoot in a shared hide. Then, with mutual hide discipline, both guns can operate only on their side (see Figure 6 overleaf). Provided that both shooters are clear about the possible dangers, and exercise good hide discipline to ensure safety at all times, this can be successful, *but* only when both guns are experienced – otherwise shoot in turn.

Shooting as a team with two clearly defined arcs of fire, enforced by the central pole can be successful. The ways that work best are either for each to take it in turn to have first shot or – what I find more successful with a single bird – is to call it 'Yours' or 'Mine' depending on to whose side it is presenting the shot. If more than one bird is in range over the decoys, select the left- or right-hand bird respectively and either one person says 'One, two – three' and both fire on the count of 'Three' or, with experienced partners, let the person

In a shared hide note central partition to create a
safe arc of fire for each shooter

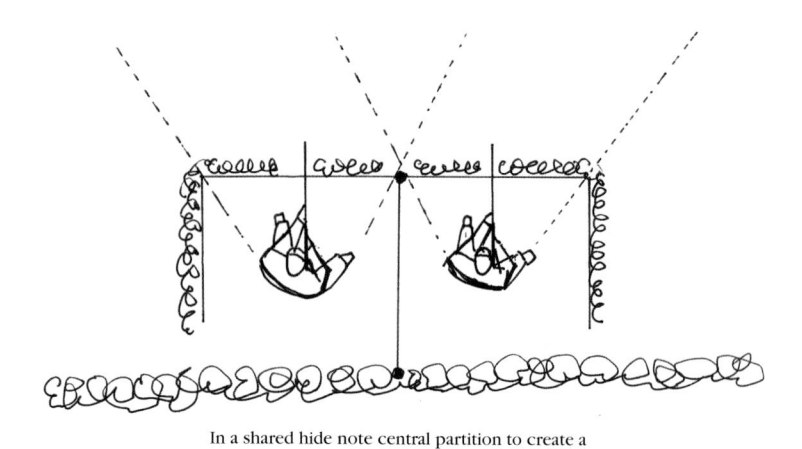

Figure 6. *Importance of a central front hide pole to maintain safety in a double hide.*

with the longer shot take his first and then the easier bird is shot a moment later. This ensures that the person with the more difficult shot selects his own timing, which usually results in a more accurate shot. When two shots are simultaneous, the teamwork can be very satisfying. However, it can only work with experienced pigeon shots otherwise the result will be two misses. If one person has rushed his shot and the other delayed, neither will result in success. If you are the experienced shot and you are sharing with someone who may be a good game or clay shot but is not used to decoying or sharing, then either call whose bird it is or let him have first shot.

I have shared a hide with a number of great pigeon shots over the years, from dear old Archie Coats to Richard Faulds who, in 2000, had just returned from Australia with his Olympic Gold Medal, and George Digweed. George was the easiest person with whom I've ever had the pleasure of sharing a hide. He just said, 'Will, you take everything within fifty yards and I'll take the rest.' It worked well and he generously allowed some to come within fifty yards for me! Actually, though it was not a big day, we made a good team on multiple shots. He and Richard Faulds were amazing at reading the line of long birds which they killed consistently, but that is why they are world champions.

So, if you share a hide, make sure you are both absolutely clear as to how your hide discipline is going to work to ensure there is no chance of either gun ever being able to point in a dangerous direction. I repeat that the only safe way is with a tall hide pole on the front of your hide between you.

Now that you are a safe and competent shot, having trained and practised on clays, and learned to handle your gun safely at all times, you are up and ready for a day out. So I will talk you through the way to read the flight of a pigeon in preparation for the shot as we share a hide.

CHAPTER 8
A DAY OUT PIGEON DECOYING TOGETHER

Reconnaissance

Basically there are two forms of reconnaissance; the first relates to finding the fields where pigeons are feeding and the second is reading the situation to produce the best shoot on that field. To find the field favoured by pigeons there is no better way than covering the ground, viewing from various vantage points, and watching for flight lines with the help of your binoculars. Two important shortcuts are first, a phone call to the farmer to see if he has noticed pigeons about and, second, to have a prior knowledge of the cropping layout and focus your attention on likely fields, depending on the season.

So let's jump into the car and drive around the farms over which I shoot locally and check out the likely fields for a shoot tomorrow. It is May and so we will focus on the last patches of winter rape on headlands or under trees where the crop was badly grazed down in the winter. Most of the field has full yellow flowers and yet some pigeons will persist in feeding on the low patches. There is a field of spring rape and two fields of peas for us to look at. Otherwise the rest of the land is wall-to-wall wheat and barley and, whether winter or spring sown, it is all green and of no interest to pigeons at this time of year, particularly since the farmer's spraying

Pigeons over the Decoys

regime has killed all weeds and volunteer rape from previous crops which could have been a food source.

We arrive at one of the winter rape fields and a few pigeons clatter out of an ash tree. I shot a reasonable bag on this low patch a week ago and it looks as if a few have come back while the rest have left it for another crop. This low area is now growing away and will be backward, but will produce a modest crop, thanks to the last shoot which killed or deterred the pigeons that would have damaged it.

We are looking round at mid to late afternoon when pigeons should be feeding; if we had come during the morning we may have seen nothing at this time of year. Each month has its own pattern of feeding times and our reconnaissance is based on that, otherwise we can get a false picture. Weather can also alter the timing; in hot weather pigeons feed later and, even as early in the year in April, no birds may be seen on a field until 4 p.m. and yet there could be a chance of shooting a hundred pigeons on it by 7.30 p.m. I have at times done that after seeing another pigeon shooter pack up at 3 p.m. He'd been there without firing a shot since 9 a.m. and given it up as a bad job. He was on the right field – just there at the wrong time.

But back to our sortie together. We are now entering the gateway of the spring rape field where I saw birds beginning to build up last week. Oh dear, the farmer has seen them too and there are two gas guns set to go off with one, two or three bangs every twenty minutes. No wonder there are no birds around. However, spring rape is such an attractive crop for pigeons that we must keep an eye on it as the birds will eventually get used to gas guns and land on the field for a quick bite and get progressively bolder as days go by. Eventually they will ignore the bangs and hardly lift into the air before landing again to feed. When this happens it may produce a good shoot as the birds will not be disturbed by the gunshots either. Then is the time to have some sport and kill a good bag, thus protecting the crop when other methods have failed.

Now we will drive to the next farm to check out the two pea fields and hope there are birds there for our shoot tomorrow. The two fields are adjacent to one another and we can see the crop is now about six inches tall. Peas can attract pigeons at nearly every stage but the young growth is particularly tasty at a time when little else is on the menu. The farmer has been chasing pigeons off these fields for several weeks and I have shot several good bags. However, in spite of my shooting and gas guns banging throughout daylight hours we can see some birds flitting here and there. We will watch from this rise in the ground where both fields are visible to us without disturbing the pigeons already feeding (see Figure 7). The likely flight lines are from the big wood to the south or the big estate to the north. Yes,

A DAY OUT PIGEON DECOYING TOGETHER

look – here is a single bird heading upwind from the north; it overflies the first field and sees movement of birds on the edge of the other, so swings to turn and swoops in to join them. Now a group of three come from the wood to the south; they seem also to know where the quiet area is to feed. Then bang-bang-bang, one of the two gas guns goes off on the far side but the birds on the opposite side barely notice: these pigeons are familiar with this form of deterrent, knowing it to be inconvenient, not life-threatening.

More birds arrive on the two lines but some drop into both fields on the quietest sides away from the gas guns. Others drop into the middle of each field. Certainly there are an encouraging number of pigeons for a shoot but let's see now how they arrive. To do this we will disturb the birds and clear the fields. We drive round the track and stop – clapping hands or tooting the horn, or even waving a white flag – whatever we need to do. Then, having sent the birds back to their respective woods, we sit and wait. The birds start to return on the lines as before and with no others to draw them by movement on the ground they have to circle round and select the preferred place to feed. Hopefully this exercise will confirm what you saw before and they will drop in on the same patches. Good, now that we have established their preferred pattern of approach and feeding areas let us consider where to erect our hide, assuming the wind will be in the same direction tomorrow. If it varies then we will need to reassess the birds' flight lines, how they approach and where they want to feed.

I like the look of the upwind field for two reasons. First, our shots will keep the downwind field disturbed and second, the focal point of the feeding was clearly the low patch by the clump of willows in the hedgerow beside

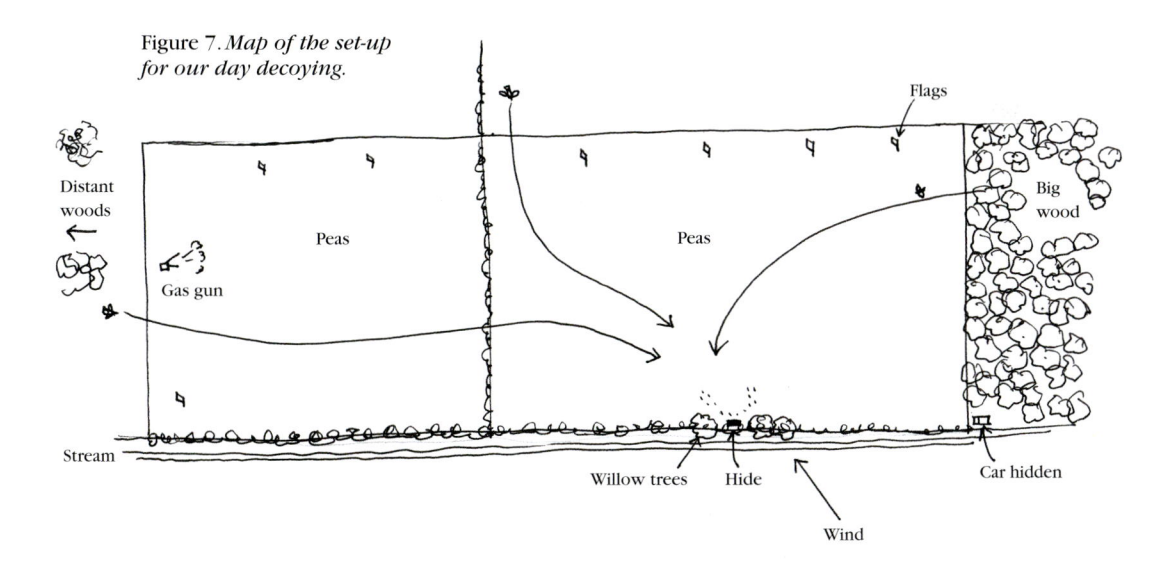

Figure 7. Map of the set-up for our day decoying.

the stream. Often a tree, or a group of them on the edge of the field, will draw birds on upwind if they cannot see their mates feeding anywhere on the field as they fly over. They will decide that the trees are a good vantage point from which to sit and watch. Therefore we will have a double reason for the pigeons coming to our chosen area for a hide; the trees and the feeding area.

However, we will have to ensure that birds do not land on the downwind field or the far side of the field we want to shoot, and so we will bring sufficient flags to keep them off those areas and hopefully steer them to us.

Now this is a good example of a typical pre-shoot reconnaissance, having first identified the potential fields and then watched carefully to assess the chosen field and make a plan of attack. This is all part of the sport and one reason why my average day produces a good bag from a field where pigeons are doing most damage, providing effective crop control for the farmer and good sport for me. Actually, I get so much pleasure and satisfaction from my reconnaissance and planning a shoot that some chums who have been with me wonder if we are ever going to set up. However, I would rather be in the right place for two hours than the wrong place for six.

So, reconnaissance is essential for consistent results and is a combination of observation, background knowledge of cropping and good networking for information with those who work on the farm. In that respect you soon learn who gives you reliable information and which farmers over-react if they see one pigeon on a crop.

A final part of pre-shooting is to phone those involved to tell them you plan to shoot next day and enquire if that is convenient and check that no agricultural activity is planned on the field. Depending on the chain of command, these people may be the owner, farm manager, foreman and certainly the keeper if the farm or estate is run with a game shoot.

If there are houses nearby, which may be disturbed by the shooting, I will contact them out of courtesy. Usually there is no problem as long as they know what is going on. Actually I am often encouraged by those with whom I speak to shoot as many pigeons as possible as they are eating the vegetables in their gardens! The key thing is diplomacy and it is important to make friends with all in the countryside.

Loading the car

Today we are making our sortie to shoot pigeons on the pea field we watched yesterday. We need to load the car with all the various bits of kit we may need for this particular field and situation. In reality it is the same as on

A DAY OUT PIGEON DECOYING TOGETHER

most outings, but I like to focus on each day to ensure that I select the right equipment. My vehicle is a 4x4 Toyota which is strong, comfortable and fitted with Goodrich All Terrain tyres. These transform any car to cope with most conditions off-road as they maintain good traction on muddy fields or slippery hill tracks. For me it is a working vehicle, doubling as my artist's studio and pigeon shooting wagon on other days. My dog, Scott, is in the back and travels with me for all activities. It does get mucked up with mud, blood and feathers but the seat covers protect the upholstery.

There is a place for everything as I load up for the day and I have a mental checklist. It is annoying to find you have forgotten something when you come to set up. If you do, don't worry – we all find we have done so on one occasion or other. For any day shooting I say 'gun' and 'cartridges' as I start the car as, without these, you are in a muddle – everything else can usually be improvised even if it is inconvenient or difficult to do so.

You will arrive at your own system but mine goes as follows. A 250 case of cartridges (two if I'm really optimistic) slips in behind the driver's seat. On top goes my small square travel bag with ear muffs, sunglasses and all the bits and pieces mentioned in Chapter 4. The light bag of artificial decoys and cradles goes on the back seat, in the middle of which is my canvas kitbag of nets. My swivel seat is loaded upturned on the rear seat behind the passenger seat. In the foot well on that side are batteries for rotaries or flappers and a box of rope bangers should they be needed. Depending on the season a suitable coat or additional clothing is bundled in and my gun then rests on top, immediately behind the front seats, protected and covered by the clothing.

In the rear section Scott has the right half, which has an old piece of carpet on which he is comfortable and in the corner is a bowl of water. It is the non-spill type which prevents water from slopping about on the journey.

On the left at the rear are various tools, such as spade, bow saw, tow rope, hammer and loppers. On top of these is my bundle of telescopic hide poles, a canvas bag with a rotary and a long, thin bag with side zip in which I have floaters and rods to fix on top of my hide poles if I need a roof. Actually the hide poles could go in this bag. Also jammed in the corner are half a dozen sacks for loading dead birds at the end of the day. You will remember what I said earlier – be optimistic and carry more cartridges and sacks than you think you will need. I then slide the flags on their long poles across the back of the front and rear seats.

Finally, in the foot well of the passenger seat if I am travelling alone, I put a plastic basket of dead birds for decoys. These are either fresh from the previous day or from the freezer, having been thawed out overnight. A tip is to put a polythene bag under these as, even if there is a rubber foot mat, when pigeons thaw out there is a certain amount of blood that leaks from them and my wife, Gina, is not surprisingly upset if we have to go out that evening in my car!

My binoculars are always ready in the storage box between the front seats and so hopefully now all is ready. Oh yes, have I remembered my coffee flask or cold drink and sandwiches in my little travel bag? Believe me, unless you are superhuman you will forget something one day. Recently while ensuring I had not forgotten to put milk and sugar in my coffee flask I found I had actually forgotten the coffee powder itself. Warm, sweet, milky water is not to be recommended! However, I did have my gun and cartridges so did shoot a bag of birds.

Arriving on the field

Being the middle of May we do not expect much action until the afternoon or early evening. We have arrived at midday as there is some work to do in preparation to optimise our chances of good sport and effective control of the pigeons we spied yesterday damaging the crop.

Yes, look, a few birds have clattered from the willows in the area where we plan to build our hide. Another small bunch scatter from one edge of the field. However, I am pleased to see so few birds already here; I hope this means that the majority are still back in the distant woods resting or socialising before flighting out to feed. This is why the previous day's reconnaissance at the time when we would expect the birds to be out feeding was so important. Otherwise we could have arrived before the birds came to feed, seen few and gone to try to find pigeons elsewhere without knowing that there were a good number coming later.

Luckily there are farm tracks around these fields for the farmer to service the gas guns. We will drive round the upwind field and set up two or three flags on the opposite side from where we are to shoot. This will hopefully keep birds off that area. There is a gas gun to scare birds but I will disconnect it as we do not want the bangs to disturb pigeons flying to our decoys. The flags will keep them on the wing moving towards us.

However, we will leave the gas gun working on the downwind field and put flags at strategic points to do all that we can to prevent pigeons landing there. I hope that they will then overfly upwind to our field where we plan to decoy them. This may all sound like unnecessary hard work but careful thought, planning and preparation of the day based on reconnaissance is the secret to making good bags. Without this we may get some shooting but not

A DAY OUT PIGEON DECOYING TOGETHER

optimise the situation, as the pigeons would soon learn to avoid us and start to land elsewhere on one of the two fields. They would then draw other birds and before you know it there would be a large flock feeding on the other field while we are in 'cold' corner.

Where to leave the vehicle

Right, so the stage is set except for the final strategic positioning of the vehicle, which we will do after unloading and setting up. The car can be useful as pigeons will avoid it even more than the flags and so it can be used effectively to keep birds away from other trees or from landing on another headland. But this is not always the case and there are situations when the opposite strategy is needed and the car must be hidden so birds will not be spooked by it. Every situation is different and sometimes, even if the car is parked at a distance, the sun moving round can reflect on a windscreen or rear window when it reaches a certain angle in the sky. If this reflection is then seen by birds on their approaching flight line they will be frightened away. Therefore, be aware of this and if pigeons suddenly stop responding to the decoys consider this as a possible reason.

Building the hide

A single hide amongst willows on a field edge - the same as our double hide with a second hide adjacent.

WILL'S PIGEON SHOOTING

If in shadow, a simple net hide will be sufficient – alert and watching. (Charles Sainsbury-Plaice)

A pigeon approaches from the right. (Charles Sainsbury-Plaice)

The moment of killability as it passes over the decoys. (Charles Sainsbury-Plaice)

The shot is taken, the bird is killed as the gun swings through the line. (Charles Sainsbury-Plaice)

The bird crumples dead. (Charles Sainsbury-Plaice)

And so another in the bag. (Charles Sainsbury-Plaice)

A DAY OUT PIGEON DECOYING TOGETHER

A great deal has been written about building hides and there are no limits to the variations depending on the circumstances. The questions to ask yourself are: 'How can I best hide myself in this particular situation?' 'What will look so natural to a pigeon that it will not question the structure or see me inside it?' That all sounds good common sense but so often one sees a dark square net hide set up in a field or on a field's edge. If it looks like a pigeon hide to you or me from half a mile away it will certainly also look like that to any half-experienced woodpigeon. Because you have purchased four poles and a bundle of camouflaged netting that does not mean you will somehow immediately become invisible. There is no magic wand and the illusion only exists in your mind. The poles and netting are the start of a successful hide, not the finish. Only if you are making a hide in a hedgerow, perhaps in the shade of a tree on a sunny day, will you get away with just a net. But in that case it is more the shadow than the net that is hiding you.

I am not denying that there are some circumstances when a net hide without foliage to help it blend into the natural surroundings will be effective. This can work when in shadow, as suggested, or if the netting is a particularly good match with the background in colour and tone. It may also work if you are shooting in an area where pigeons are not regularly shot and so are more easily fooled by decoys and a less than perfect hide. For the same reason young birds, being inexperienced, will respond well to any decoys. Finally there are days when even the most wary of pigeons are so keen on the food available that they will throw themselves at the decoys in pure greed. However, in many parts of Britain this is rare as, with the ever-increasing number of pigeon shooters, the birds become so wary that many will just flare off or pass by without responding to your carefully arranged decoys if your hide does not look natural.

So, to build a successful hide:

1. Site the hide where the pigeons want to feed, not where it is just easy and convenient to do so. Don't be lazy and take the easy option. If carrying your kit out into the middle of a field could be more successful, do it; otherwise you may miss a good shoot and sit all day regretting it.
2. Whatever the construction of the hide, ensure that it looks as natural as possible in the landscape.
3. Make it large enough to be comfortable. I start from the inside and build around my seat, cartridge case, bag, etc. rather than building a hide and then trying to cram everything in.
4. Make the back of the hide taller than the front so that when you rise to shoot you are not silhouetted. Otherwise you will appear to pigeons

like a jack-in-the-box and the birds will flare and make a shot difficult or impossible.
5. The front of the hide should be high enough to conceal you but low enough to shoot over. Make sure you can see through the front of the hide to watch oncoming birds, not just over the top, or you will be visible.
6. Put a top on the hide if pigeons are expected to approach from behind so they do not see you from above.
7. If constructing a hide in the open on a day with a strong wind be prepared to use one or more guy ropes to prevent the hide blowing over.

Thought should be given to the angle of shots likely to be experienced. If pigeons are expected to decoy well, then most shooting will be at a low, flat trajectory. However, in other circumstances, if near trees for instance, you will experience high overhead shots. You must then be careful that the bird cannot see into the hide as it approaches from a height. This may mean you will need to have a roof or cover over all or part of the hide. In some cases I will have a tall branch up one side of the hide, behind which I can keep hidden for a bird to be shot above and yet also be able to take on those which decoy out in front of the hide.

Bale hides

A good, round bale hide as made by Andy Hill in Aberdeenshire.

There will be occasions when the pigeons are feeding out in the middle of a big field and a hide is needed away from any surrounding hedge, fence or trees. This is best done by building a hide a few days before you wish to shoot, but often that is not possible. Some years ago it was easy to arrange for the helpful farmer to take straw bales to your chosen spot. Archie Coats had a good design for this form of hide based on fourteen bales – three each for the walls at front and sides and four at the back with one for a seat. To fine-tune the height one could have some bales on their sides rather than flat, which then raised the sides or back as required. However, those small bales are a thing of the past on most farms. The large jumbo-sized round or square bales weighing half a ton are what we see in fields today after the corn is cut. If shooting on stubble it is easy to make a net hide against a square bale, or to roll three round ones together with one at each side and the other at the back. This, with a net front and a roof covered with loose straw found on the field, is cosy and accepted totally by the pigeons.

Bush hides

If no bales are available then pigeons will surprisingly accept a new bush in the landscape even if it is in the middle of an open field. Therefore a net hide surrounded by leafy branches will work well. It took me some time to have

A bush hide erected out in a stubble field – note the high back to the hide.

WILL'S PIGEON SHOOTING

With hide poles in position, the camouflaged netting is hung around the hide.
(Don Brunt)

Natural vegetation is added.
(Don Brunt)

The completed hide. Pigeons will accept a new bush in the open field.
(Don Brunt)

With tall branches behind and on each side the pigeons cannot see you as they approach. (Don Brunt)

Whilst being well hidden there is a good window through which to shoot over the decoys in front of the hide.
(Don Brunt)

Picking up at the end of a successful day. (Don Brunt)

106

the courage to do this as, although it was necessary to be out in the field where the birds wanted to feed, I felt very exposed. A tip to help transport a bunch of selected branches cut with either a bow saw or loppers is to have a short length of thin rope. This has a loop on each end and, having stacked the butts of the branches together, just pass one end around them and, having passed the other end through the loop, pull it tight. Then put a hitch around the bundle again and loop the free end over the tow bar or rear bumper of your vehicle. The bundle can then be dragged into place. This is easy at the beginning of the day and again at the end when clearing up and the branches can be hidden underneath a hedge out of the way of agricultural machinery. In winter when the trees are bare you can take out branches of conifer – Leylandii is ideal as it lies flat and is easily bundled. Pigeons seem to accept this suburban addition to the natural countryside.

Umbrella hides

In some standing crops like peas or corn you can use an angler's umbrella as the basis for a hide. When set up on its side, back to the wind, it can be stable especially if guy ropes are angled out behind and pegged to the ground. Then, with camo nets over the top and across the front, a hide is easily erected. You then cover this with the stems of the surrounding crop, which are obviously an exact match to the whole field. You will need a low seat for this form of hide and it is cramped, with an arc of fire limited to the front only. However, I have shot many big bags of pigeons from this simple form of instant hide. Obviously it is ideal in bad weather when a wet day can be uncomfortable and so I usually have my green angler's umbrella in the car for such occasions. In the rain it can also be used to make a cosy dry hide beside a hedgerow or under a tree. A shower will stop pigeons feeding temporarily, but if the weather is wet all day the birds must feed sometime and will do so regardless of the rain. I can recall a number of very good days shooting when the rain never stopped but sitting under the umbrella I was dry – though packing up at the end of a wet day is not fun, with sodden nets and soggy pigeons to load into sacks.

One day, shooting on peas in summer when the rain never eased, I was amazed to suddenly see a fox working up the field having scented my decoys and dead birds in front of the hide. It trotted right up to me and I shot it. An hour later another did the same thing with a similar result, which pleased the keeper of the shoot. The wet weather must have given those foxes a false sense of security believing that all humans would be indoors – well, all sensible ones were!

One sees various forms of tent-like camouflaged hides advertised in the shooting press. They are mostly based on American duck blinds and I'm sure they could be very successful but I have never used one. They are popular with wildlife photographers who only need a small hole through which to film, and most designs seem to have an even more limited arc of fire than the angler's umbrella.

Double hides

We have talked about double hides when discussing the safe way for two people to shoot together. In my view the best way to make a hide for two people is to build what, in effect, are two single hides side by side. This structure then has a partition between the two shooters, which creates two important benefits and yet does not prevent conversation and camaraderie. The first benefit is that, if the hide does not have a roof, the central screen obscures the second Gun when a high pigeon comes in from the side – see Figure 8. Second, the most important benefit of the central partition is that there is a pole supporting it at the front of the hide that prevents swinging the gun over your partner. Each shooter will have his own window through which to shoot safely. Ideally then only one Gun shoots at a time, both taking it in turns or perhaps changing after every ten shots.

I will digress a little here from the description of the day to explain that, if there are two experienced Guns in a double hide it can work well to both shoot as long as a tight discipline is followed. A single bird is taken by the Gun on whichever side the bird presents a shot. If two birds arrive together, then each Gun takes the bird on their side and they ideally shoot at the same time – to assist this, either count one, two, three bang or both get to know your respective timing so that the shots are fired simultaneously. If successful

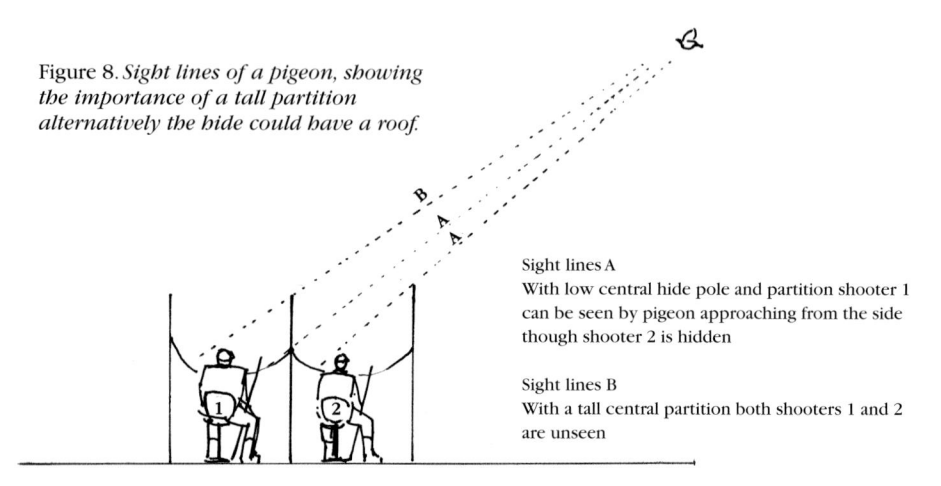

Figure 8. *Sight lines of a pigeon, showing the importance of a tall partition alternatively the hide could have a roof.*

Sight lines A
With low central hide pole and partition shooter 1 can be seen by pigeon approaching from the side though shooter 2 is hidden

Sight lines B
With a tall central partition both shooters 1 and 2 are unseen

A DAY OUT PIGEON DECOYING TOGETHER

it is very satisfactory to kill two birds simultaneously. However, this takes practice and if it does not work then it is best to let one Gun try for a right and left in turn (see later). If the synchronised shooting works and good teamwork is achieved then four birds can, at times, be shot. This is more difficult than it sounds and usually two people sharing a hide do not shoot with as good a cartridge average as when shooting alone. This is because either your own timing of a shot is compromised or you are chasing a bird which has been spooked by the other person's shot. However, shooting in company with a friend to share the day is always great fun, *but always be constantly aware to ensure safe shooting at all times*. Occasionally one reads of a tragic accident when two people were pigeon shooting together, so please ensure you do not become a statistic – enjoy your shooting together safely.

Reverting to construction, in all other aspects a double hide should follow the guidelines for building a single hide, just that it will be twice the size.

So today, to shoot the field of peas, we will make a double hide near the willows on the western side of the field. The obvious position is to build a hide under the trees for additional cover, on the assumption that you will be shooting some birds which may be coming to the trees rather than to the decoys out in the field. However, when deciding the exact spot it is a good idea to stand in the chosen position and look out to check what actual field of view you have to shoot. If a tree is large and wide-spreading it can obstruct your view of approaching birds just at the point you want to shoot them (see Figure 9). In that case it is a good idea to be along the hedge to one side of the tree, then you can shoot a high bird without it disappearing behind the

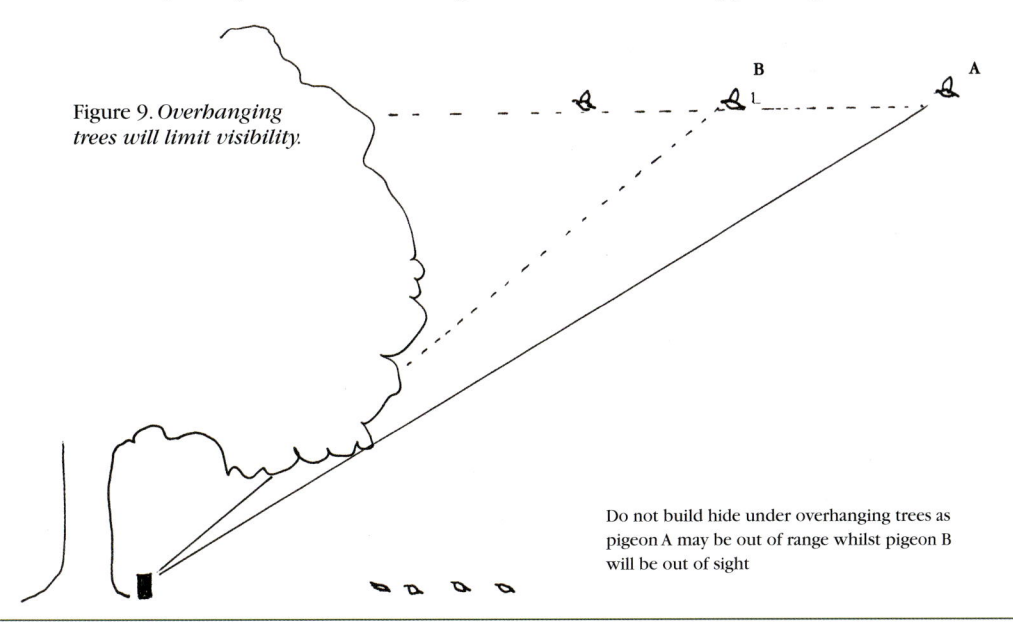

Figure 9. *Overhanging trees will limit visibility.*

Do not build hide under overhanging trees as pigeon A may be out of range whilst pigeon B will be out of sight

foliage. If there is a cross-wind you should build the hide on the downwind side of the trees as that will be the side from which the pigeons approach.

As the wind is westerly today and so coming from behind us, we will be shooting the birds approaching from the front. Therefore I like the look of the hedge between the two willows. From there we will cover birds going to either tree with a full arc of fire to optimise our chances. However, we will need to build the sides of the hide fairly tall or we will be visible to birds approaching high from either side. The hedge is tall enough at the back of the hide to prevent us being seen by birds that come from behind.

First we will place each seat in position, checking that the ground is level; if it isn't we'll dig or chip with the spade until it is flat. Then we place the cartridges and bag of kit into position next to your seat, which will be the one on the left as we look out to the field, because you say you are not so good on your right. This is normal because a right-handed shot can swing the gun more naturally to the left than to the right. The next stage is to press the telescopic hide poles into the ground using the kick plates at the bottom to ensure the points are firmly in the soil and the poles are solid enough to support the netting and foliage that we then put around the framework. Backed by the tall hedge we do not need a net behind us, but must ensure that the sides and central partition are high enough to prevent us from being seen. The front is high enough to hide us but low enough to shoot over comfortably. The central pole is at full height between us to ensure a gun projecting forward for a shot can never swing into the other person's space.

The elder branches we have collected are propped around the outside of the hide and can be clipped onto the poles with clamp spring clips. Final adjustment is made when we are inside the hide sitting down and the height of the netting and pruning of twigs can be attended to.

Setting out decoys

It is always a good idea to keep fifteen or twenty dead birds in the freezer to use as decoys next time one gets a chance to get out for a day's shooting. Remember to get them out the night before! Today we have fifteen in a plastic basket ready for use. A lot has been written about decoy patterns but before explaining about the different layouts in more detail I would emphasise that each is just a guide and only on the day can you assess how birds react and adjust your pattern by observing their behaviour. The object of the exercise is simple, though many books make it complicated. There are two objectives:

A DAY OUT PIGEON DECOYING TOGETHER

1. To create a group of decoys that will look like a natural feeding flock. Watch pigeons feeding and you will notice that they like their own space within a group, therefore place decoys at random about four or five yards apart. Also, you will notice that the stronger the wind the more aligned they will be, facing into it simply to ensure their feathers are blown along their bodies. If there is little breeze then there is no need for pigeons to be regimented into wind and they will turn this way and that while feeding. Therefore make your arrangement of decoys look natural.

2. The second objective is to have the pattern of decoys in a layout that brings the incoming birds into range in front of your hide, where they present a good opportunity of a shot. Therefore your attractive little flock of decoys needs to be centred about twenty-five to thirty yards from your hide. If the birds you shoot are then added to build up the picture they can extend either side, but if they are out beyond about thirty-five yards you will just keep getting long shots, fewer chances of rights and lefts, and fewer clean kills. So, if anything, keep your decoys closer in the hope that they will bring the decoyed pigeons well within what I call the net, i.e. the killing area. To encourage pigeons to flight to the area where you want to shoot them, leave a gap of about eight to ten yards in the middle of your decoys as this open space will encourage pigeons to think of landing there. They do not like to land among a dense group.

Bring in dead birds that have fallen beyond your decoy pattern. (Charles Sainsbury-Plaice)

If the pigeons are decoying well, one can steer them to a chosen area to optimise results. However, this only works with either inexperienced young pigeons or where others have not been spooked frequently, becoming wary of decoys and pigeon shooters. Usually you just have to be pleased to have drawn them into range wherever they make a shot.

Wind direction

Let us look now at the different wind directions and how we can best steer pigeons into the killing zone.

Wind from behind (Figure 10). This is ideal as pigeons will approach from the front upwind. In this case a horseshoe shape can work well with a few decoys across the front only about ten to fifteen yards from the hide, with others fanning out and making a group either side of the killing area.

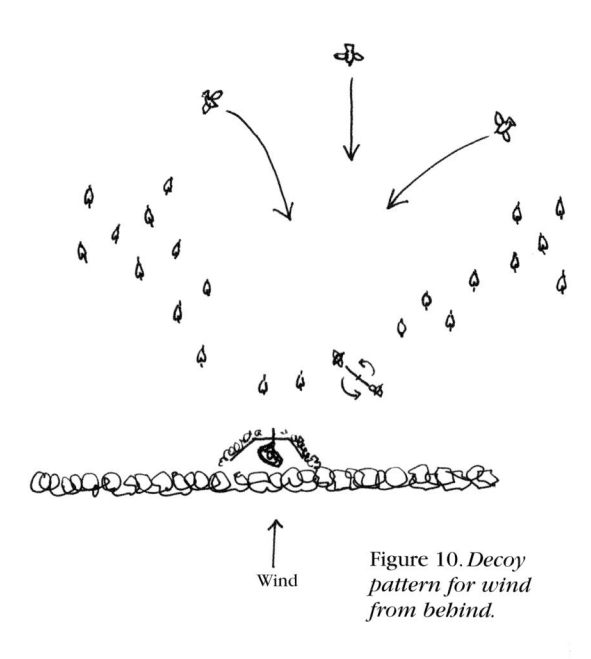

Figure 10. *Decoy pattern for wind from behind.*

Side wind (Figure 11). Make a crescent shape of decoys on the upwind side

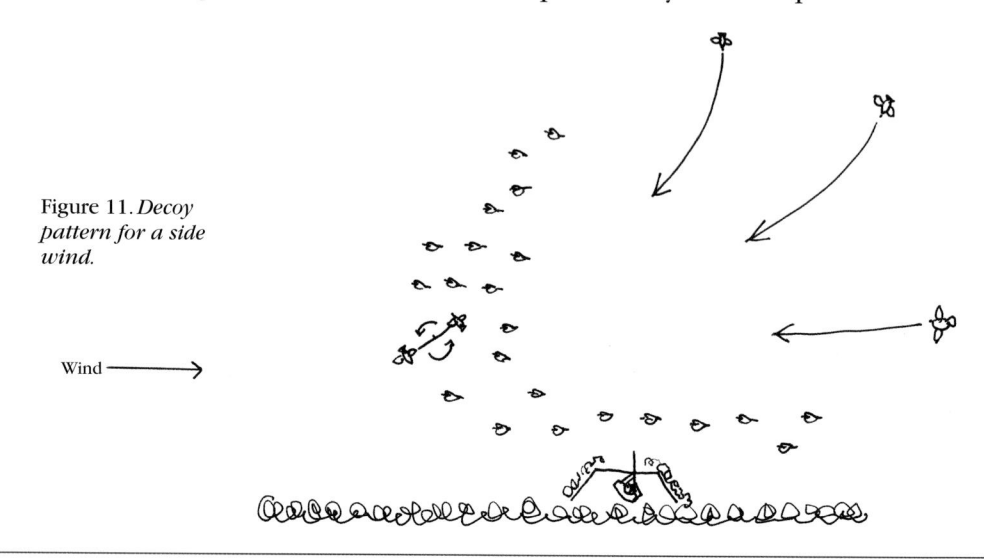

Figure 11. *Decoy pattern for a side wind.*

A DAY OUT PIGEON DECOYING TOGETHER

in front of your hide. The pigeons will then approach from the downwind side, flying upwind across the front of your hide where your killing area will be.

Wind is in your face (Figure 12). This is not ideal but there are conditions when one cannot arrange to shoot any other way. Your decoys can be set up in a crescent further out at, say, forty yards or more as the pigeons will have to approach from behind you or from the side, but will be between you and the decoys, presenting going away shots. This can work very well and provided you are well hidden the pigeons will pass quite close to the hide as they come from behind and often as you shoot the first bird the second will hold in the wind for a moment, not knowing whether to continue upwind away from danger or fly downwind towards where it heard the shot. That second of indecision can be the moment of truth when you can shoot it successfully. So a position with the wind in your face, while not being the preferred one, can produce success and I can recall a number of surprisingly good days when it worked well.

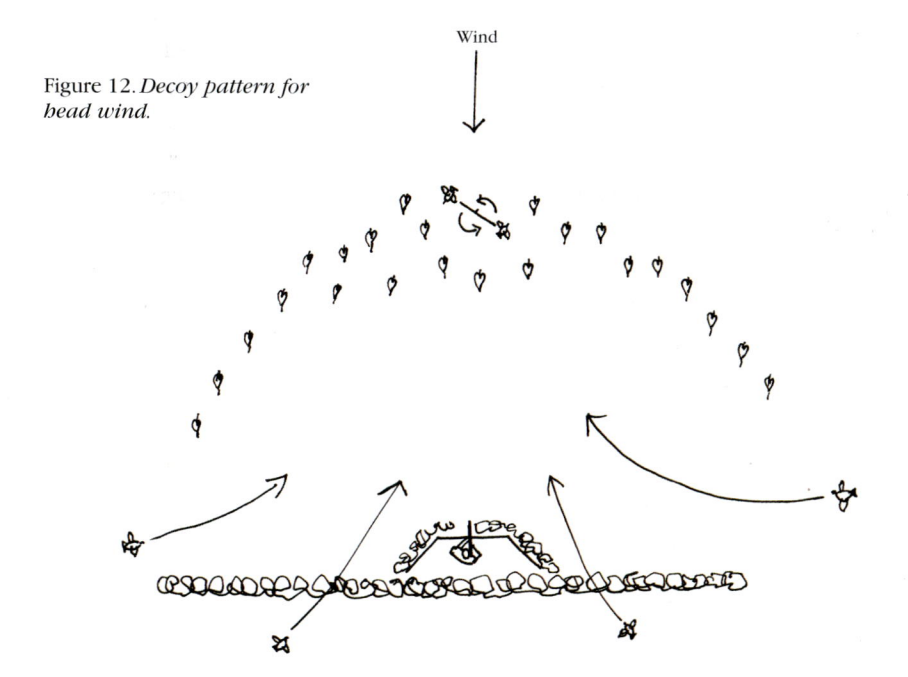

Figure 12. *Decoy pattern for head wind.*

Today we have the wind behind us and will start with a pattern as per Figure 10. So, with the basket of dead birds we walk out from the hide and toss them roughly into position with a group to the left, another to the right and one or two in between the groups, about fifteen to twenty yards out from

WILL'S PIGEON SHOOTING

Tossing dead pigeon decoys into position to create a random and natural layout (in this case on a stubble). (Rupert Watts)

the hide. The peas are about six to eight inches tall and, to lift the decoys and make them more visible, we will set them up on wire cradles. The wind is not strong but just a steady breeze, which is ideal, therefore the decoys can be set generally facing the wind but some are angled left and others to the right, just as a natural group of pigeons would feed. Some people set pigeons with their heads up in the air but it is best to keep the bird with its neck and head parallel with the ground, which is the feeding angle of a pigeon. The head-up posture indicates a bird suspecting danger – not the message you want to give. Just remember the objective is to create a natural group of happily feeding pigeons.

Setting up a dead bird as a decoy on a cradle. (Rupert Watts)

Rotary decoys

As the peas are tall enough to hide pigeons on the ground we will use a rotary today. Pigeons coming to the field will be looking for movement to attract them to the place where their mates are feeding. I know we have lifted our static decoys on cradles to make them more visible, but movement will be the sign the newly arriving birds will be looking for and, as it is quite a large field, it will help draw them to our decoys.

The actual position of the rotary in relation to the decoy pattern is important. Ideally the rotary should catch the eye of a pigeon flying over the field but then, as the bird approaches upwind, it should see the static decoys and decide to join them. Therefore the rotary needs to be on the upwind side of the pattern. I have a theory that if pigeons have experienced a rotary before they are still attracted by the two birds whirling round but, as they get closer, they suddenly believe that instead of preparing to land these birds have been frightened and are actually making a rapid exit. Therefore the leading bird of an incoming group may just come into shot, but if you do not shoot it quickly it will suddenly turn away taking the others with it, without giving a chance of a shot. Each day is different and you must try different positions for the best result. If pigeons have not seen a rotary before they will come right to it and may even hover over it making easy shooting, but they soon learn and can become very shy of these machines.

Today we will set it up on the upwind side of the right-hand group of decoys to start with. Make sure the base is firmly into the ground or the movement will soon shake it loose. My preferred angle is to tilt it so the circle of the moving birds is not parallel to the ground. It may make no difference but I feel they are more visible. Also, I tilt each bird on its supporting cradle with the inner wing down to give the appearance of them swinging in to land.

Some rotaries have variable speeds and as a rule it seems to work best when the speed is related to that of the wind. So if there is little wind then set a slow speed, but full speed in a good breeze. An average speed of 45rpm works best.

Whatever size or form of battery you use it is wise to hide it with natural vegetation, straw or clods of soil, depending on what is available on the field.

With decoys in place and the rotary working we now ensure all our kit is in place in the hide. The car will be hidden under the trees in the wood to our right. It may be necessary later to use it as part of our flag system to keep birds off an area of the field or to steer a line of pigeons to us. However, that will become obvious later, should we need to reposition it.

The dog

My dog, Scott, a friendly golden retriever, can come with us today as he can be hidden under the hedge near one of the willows well away from our hide. In that way he will be able to help retrieve wounded birds, but not be close enough for the shooting to damage his hearing. To avoid this I leave him in the car until after the shoot unless he can be hidden away from the hide. As there is a stream behind the willows he will not need his water bowl, otherwise it is important to ensure a dog always has access to water. A dog naturally wants to be with you and it takes time to train one to sit or lie hidden at a distance from you. However, a young dog started off on a lead pegged down in the position where you want him to stay will soon learn. It can help to put a sack for the dog to lie on, which also emphasises the exact position to stay. Scott has many faults but he is very steady in position and after a retrieve I just say 'In you get' while pointing, and off he goes into position and lies down with just his nose pointing out to watch.

The stage is set

Now we can settle into the hide and hopefully wait for action. We can be optimistic as the conditions are good, with fine weather and a steady breeze. We saw birds here yesterday afternoon and they should come to feed today. It is now 1 p.m. and it has taken nearly an hour to get everything in place and set up. The first birds will probably come to the willow trees as they have all afternoon to feed and so are in no hurry. The main feeding time should be between about 4 p.m. until 7 p.m. at this time of year, but we are set up ready for any that arrive early. However, action will not be brisk for an hour or two so now we have a good chance to nibble at our sandwiches.

Taking the first shots

There are a few birds moving about over the wood to our right but they are just socialising. Ah – now – there are two pigeons coming from the woods to our left, flying over the downwind field – yes, they are coming on and are now over our field and they are swinging right-handed towards our side, probably to come and sit in the trees. One drifts away but the other has seen the decoys and is coming to the willow on your side. Keep still – he closes his wings and drifts down towards the top of the tree. You put your gun up but in a flash the bird sees you and with the flick of a wing is away downwind and your shot at a disappearing, jinky pigeon is optimistic. So next time prepare for the shot earlier, with gun held pointing up towards where you anticipate to take the shot as the bird approaches the tree. In this way you will need minimal movement to mount and shoot. Until that moment you must keep still, concealed behind your side of the hide.

A DAY OUT PIGEON DECOYING TOGETHER

Here comes a single bird on the same line. Good, he's not seen you and now – up – mount the gun and shoot. Yes, good shot and that bird never knew you were there and so presented a shot on a line and at a speed you could read well, resulting in a dead pigeon at the base of the tree.

These three pigeons coming from the right look likely customers. Yes, the leader has seen the decoys and the others are following. These are dropping into the decoys. You stand up and take a long shot without success as the three birds scatter away downwind. It is not easy to judge the right moment to take a shot, and jumping up too soon is a common fault. Try letting the birds, or at least one, come well into range. If it has not seen you it will sometimes come very close. It is easy to let it go further away, but once you show yourself it will never come nearer. Therefore control the excitement and wait whilst crouched down behind the front of the net or foliage of the hide. Keep absolutely still and only when the pigeon looks to be an easy shot do you slowly rise to shoot. The bird will probably still be further away than you think, and will actually not be as easy as it appeared. Try to get the timing of up-two-three-bang as the gun is raised, mounted, bird engaged and shot taken.

Now here is another single bird circling as it comes from behind before approaching upwind to the decoys. It comes closer – good, you are keeping down and hidden and not moving. The bird comes well into the killing area; you rise in a calm, controlled way, raise the gun and 'bang' – the bird drops dead. A perfect example of a pigeon that decoyed well and was then killed cleanly. Just a puff of white feathers drifting away on the wind to tell the tale.

Another pigeon is added to the bag. (Rupert Watts)

I like to think of the area which is in range out over the decoys as the 'net'. Therefore let the bird come well into the net and it will give you the chance of a sensible shot. This is even more important if there is more than one pigeon, providing a possible right and left when you judge two birds to be in the net. We will get a chance of this during the afternoon if birds continue to come to the decoys.

Another pigeon comes to the tree and you make another good shot. You are obviously comfortable with the birds making a right to left shot, which is a right-hander's natural swing.

Shooting from a sitting position

Here is one coming to the tree on my side, the right-hand of the hide. Because it will make a left to right shot for me I will swivel round on my seat to face further to the right than the position from which I anticipate taking the shot. In that way I will swing into a comfortable body angle. The bird comes on and makes a straightforward shot. Had I still been facing the front, the stretch round to my right would have been beyond the comfortable swing. As a result the shot would probably have gone low as my right shoulder and gun rolled below the line of the bird. So Figures 4 and 5 (see pages 91 and 92) show a useful tip on getting the correct angle to allow your swing to be into, rather than out from, your comfortable body position.

Communing with Nature

The afternoon soon passes with a few shots and then a lull. Even then there is always something in Nature to observe – what are those small birds passing along the hedge? Is that a hobby that flashed past hunting a dragonfly? A comma butterfly on the flowers of the whitethorn, so appropriately called May blossom? A plant here or insect there – never is there a dull moment when sitting in a pigeon hide. I am sorry for those for whom a day is only as good as the number of birds in the bag, or shots fired. There have been many quiet days but, even on a day when it never stopped raining and hardly a pigeon crossed the horizon and the most exciting thing was a snail slowly creeping across my case of cartridges, there was always optimism that the rain would stop and pigeons pour out to feed – actually they did and my companion had packed up and gone home, but I sat it out and had a brisk hour's sport and shot a sackful of pigeons.

Communing with Nature is good for the soul and many of our country sports are fulfilling for that reason. This is appreciated by the angler huddled under his umbrella beside the river or the stalker waiting for a stag to stand for the shot, or a roe to show while on a high seat as dawn breaks. The heart of the hunter runs parallel with Mother Nature and Father Time.

Extending the decoy pattern

With about a dozen shot birds on the ground we will go out and set them up to expand the original pattern of decoys. The wind has backed from westerly to south-westerly and so we will put more birds on the upwind side beyond where the rotary is positioned. This will hopefully keep steering the incoming birds to the killing zone in front of our hide.

You have had some good shots when your timing was right and with experience you will learn to read the flight of incoming birds to anticipate the moment of optimum killability. Often this is the moment when the pigeon turns side on, or head on, depending on the wind. That is when shots are possible at fully committed pigeons coming to decoys. Often, the moment is more difficult to read as the bird is in the net but not thinking of landing, just flying over and then veering away, being not fully convinced about the decoy pattern. Such birds need judging carefully and the flight will usually offer a shot when the line and speed hold steady for just long enough to make one sensibly. Only with experience can you learn to read and see this point of flight. This is how an experienced pigeon shot can achieve a good kill to cartridge percentage. A pigeon jinking about, twisting and turning, is only going to create a speculative chance, usually resulting in a miss. An American I knew referred to such birds as 'yinking and yanking' which, whilst being two nonsense words, strangely describe the approach flight of a pigeon so well.

Rights and lefts

Now, back in the hide, we can see more birds moving about across the sky and there is more of a sense of purpose to their flight. Here are two coming in and a chance of a right and left. Let them come well into the net and take the further bird first – 'bang-bang'. Well done, you killed the longer bird but were just behind the other as it jinked, turned and was off in the blink of an eye. It's not easy to kill rights and lefts consistently unless you are decoying on a tall crop like a patch of laid corn or well-grown peas. Then, if the birds are responding well, you can let one land in the crop where it is out of sight and shoot the second bird as it arrives. When the first bird lifts to fly away it is confused as to where the shot came from and will often hold position in the air before flying off. In that way you can kill both birds without either of them ever seeing your movement, which results in more steady shots. So to kill rights and lefts ensure that two birds are well within range. Try to shoot the further one first to give the best chance of the second still being in range as it flies off. Do not hurry the second shot but learn to read the position of both birds you are trying to shoot, so when the first is killed you immediately know where to swing onto the second.

Sometimes there may be a flock of pigeons over the decoys and it is easy to be flustered when spoilt for choice, but again try to select your two birds before you shoot the first and disregard all the others. If you shoot one and then try to find a second of a group you will be confused and pick one, then change and end up with nothing. I know – I have done it too often!

Sitters

We have shot several more that have come flying to the willows either side. More are now decoying well as they are more intent on feeding. One comes and lands just as it is in range but before you can shoot it flying. I suggest you shoot it on the ground – although this is not a sporting shot you must remember that we are here to help the farmer protect his crop, therefore we owe it to the farmer to kill any pigeons that visit the field. We are having many very exciting and sporting shots at birds as they come at all speeds, heights and angles, but occasionally we must forsake a sporting shot for one that is doing the deed to protect the crop. We are not on a pheasant shoot where one leaves the low ones and only selects the ones flying at a sporting height.

Killing wounded birds humanely

One or two of our shot birds were just winged and, having landed, started to walk off. We have quickly nipped out of the hide to pick the bird and dispatch it. There are a number of ways of doing this but the method I find quickest and most humane is to hold the bird across its back in my left hand and its head between forefinger and second finger of my right hand. I then hold it across my knee and stretch the neck whilst twisting upwards. This double action breaks the neck instantly and although the bird will twitch and flutter

A DAY OUT PIGEON DECOYING TOGETHER

A dog like Scott loves to be handled out for the long retrieves. (Charles Sainsbury-Plaice)

with the reaction of nerves, it is dispatched very fast with that one spontaneous action. This method needs a little practice but can soon be achieved. Actually, you can practise on a dead bird just to dislocate the neck in the way described so that, when dealing with a wounded one, there is no mistake. What is not desirable is to hold the bird by the neck and swing it round as, although the neck may be dislocated, the weight of the bird relative to the thin neck often means that the head comes off and blood spurts all over your clothes.

For longer wounded birds my dog, Scott, loves a distant retrieve and has learned to be handled out for several hundred yards – not to field trial standard but useful to ensure that all wounded birds are accounted for as quickly as possible. We have a duty to dispatch any wounded birds and pick up as thoroughly as possible.

Tidying up and awaiting evening

So how is our day going – we have now killed several more birds and it is time to unload our guns and go to tidy up the pattern again. You gather the long birds lying far out to the left and I will pick up those to the right. Scott will pick up that winged bird which came down eighty yards out. Our pattern now has about sixty pigeons, with the shot birds added to the original decoys. We will keep the central patch open as the incoming birds will still come to that area where there appears to be an easy landing gap without competition. By gathering the long birds we will prevent incomers trying to land too far out as was beginning to happen. This can only lead to shooting birds at extreme range, which creates a greater chance of wounding.

It is now 6 p.m. and the pigeons are really active, coming on both lines from either side. The flags and rope bangers are successfully keeping the birds off the other field. Our shooting is keeping new arrivals in the air and they are continuing to come upwind until they see our decoys. We are enjoying good sport and have established a rhythm of good teamwork.

Getting back in the zone

We have killed some long, memorable shots but missed some easy ones – we all do. However, if you go through a bad patch take a lesson from top competition clay shots. Focus fully on each target as if it is the only one – visualise killing it – never take your eye off the bird until you have taken the shot with full concentration. If you miss, do not dwell on it. Think of all the ones you have killed successfully; forget the one missed.

The usual problem is that you are out decoying for four to five hours, maybe longer, and maintaining concentration is not easy. So anticipate that this may happen and do not beat yourself up if your performance suddenly becomes erratic. Have confidence that you can and will come through it. Over the years I have trained myself to pace my energy and concentration like a long-distance runner. However, on occasions when the gun and I seem to stop being as one, to get back on track I try just concentrating on one bird and I reduce the range at which I take birds on. In other words, shoot a few easier ones to build the confidence again and usually focus and concentration can be restored.

The trouble with shooting is that the brain likes to take the credit for a successful shot. You see a bird – your brain says 'Give three feet of lead' – you do and the bird crumples – brain is satisfied. However, your natural reactions are usually so much more accurate than those produced by conscious thought. If someone throws you an object you instinctively put out your hand at the right moment, at the right height and distance and judge its weight so that you can catch it comfortably. All is done so spontaneously that whether it's a tennis ball, cricket ball, apple or orange you can catch it without conscious thought entering into the equation of eye, mind, muscle co-ordination.

A DAY OUT PIGEON DECOYING TOGETHER

So when a bird flits across a gap in the trees, your gun goes up and the bird is killed, you are delighted and happily surprised. Your brain is not pleased though and says, 'Hang on, you did not let me tell you what to do'. The brain likes to feel that it is in control. If you are going through a bad patch you naturally look for help and the brain immediately steps in and says 'Yes, just listen to me'. It may then be placated by telling you how to deal with a few easy shots – confidence builds and then you can get back to your true natural reactions – the better one is shooting, the less one seems to think about it because those accurate co-ordinated actions are allowed to work freely. The brain goes off in a sulk, but waits to be called on again!

So we have two types of shot, the spontaneous and premeditated. The more you practise shooting any form of target, the more the experience will build a pattern of mental pictures of accurate shots when an instinctive spontaneous shot is successful. Eye/muscle response is spontaneous and accurate, but adding in conscious thought opens up all sorts of computations which can lead to a miss.

Now you are back on track, shooting well after the lull of concentration, and more birds are lying dead amongst the decoys. Time for another quick tidy up and although the flow of birds is slowing we will hopefully continue with a few more shots before the end. We no longer need to add any more birds to the decoy pattern but just gather handfuls and bring them back in a pile beside the hide. A good idea is to cover them with a sack to stop any flies getting to them.

Another half hour of sport and suddenly there comes a moment when it is all over. No more birds are flighting out to feed although they are still flying around the distant woods where they will settle down to roost. Well, we've enjoyed a great day's sport.

Packing up and picking up

This is a sad part of a good day, but must be done methodically, so the foliage around the hide is dragged into the bottom of the hedge, poles collected, nets stowed in the bag, cartridge cases all cleared up (if not popped into a bag during shooting) and gun safely zipped into its sleeve, decoys gathered up and all the bits and pieces of equipment loaded back in the vehicle.

When picking up, I collect the dead birds into random piles over the area where they have fallen, ready for bagging up into sacks of forty or fifty. I then get Scott out of the car, or from where he has been sitting under a hedge or back in the wood. He will work the hedgerow or cover to retrieve birds

Picking up by hand the birds lying on the open field. (Charles Sainsbury-Plaice)

either side of the hide. Then we will take a wide circle and pick up the birds that have dropped a long way out from the hide. Hand-picking those birds lying around the decoys saves Scott's energy for the birds I cannot easily retrieve, and it is confusing for any dog to retrieve from among many lying in the open. A dog wants to hunt and retrieve, not be over-faced with too many, or he will tend to become confused, picking one and then dropping it to pick up another.

Remember to be careful not to let a dog damage a standing crop. Serious damage can be done when picking up on a field of swathed oilseed rape when the pods become dry and so brittle that the least disturbance causes them to burst and shed the valuable seed.

The other time to limit, or even not use a dog at all, is from April to June in areas where there is game nesting. It is difficult enough to protect game and their eggs from vermin at that time and the gamekeeper will not be pleased to find you hunting a dog up a hedge for a pigeon that you thought might be picked. Respect everything and everyone's interest in the countryside.

There is, of course, a balance to be achieved as it is important to pick up as many of your birds as possible. It is unethical to shoot and not take time to make a serious effort to retrieve as many birds as is feasible. They are all good food.

A DAY OUT PIGEON DECOYING TOGETHER

Later the dogs hunt the surrounding cover to complete a successful pick-up.
(Charles Sainsbury-Plaice)

That said, at this stage, if the weather is warm, it is important to check for fly eggs. This is not a problem before April or after October, nor on cold or windy days in summer. However there are occasions, especially on the sheltered side of a wood or hedge in summer, when fly-blown birds can be a serious problem. The eggs are easily seen with the naked eye, being cream-coloured, sausage-shaped and approximately two millimetres long. The main areas selected by bluebottles to lay their eggs are in the beaks, vents or under the wings. However any obvious bloody wound will be worth checking. To de-fly it is easy to pull off and discard the head, but other areas need plucking as the eggs are laid on the feathers surrounding the vulnerable places. If you can do this in the field before bagging them up it is easier to see them in the daylight and minimises the problem. Occasionally a bird is so covered in eggs that it must be rejected.

So, after checking for fly eggs we will bag up the dead birds, counting them into sacks. The original frozen decoys are kept separate and can be used again, but must not be offered for sale either with the fresh birds or if refrozen.

You put fifty into one sack and I will see if we have enough for another. Actually yes, and a few more, so we have a hundred – a special day indeed of good sport shared.

Just before leaving the site of the hide it is always worth a final check to see that nothing has been left. It is easy to overlook a green hide pole or hank of camo netting as everything is designed not to be seen!

All we must do now, having loaded everything into the car, is retrace our steps to collect the flags we set out at the beginning of the day. Also we must remember to reconnect the gas gun we turned off.

As we pass the farmer's house on the way out we will pop in to thank him and report on the successful day – and offer him some birds if he and his family enjoy eating pigeons.

Arriving home

Even if the kit is to be left in the car for another day there are a number of important jobs to see to. First, I go into the house to put the kettle on and prepare Scott's meal. He then comes to the kennel where he tucks in.

It is important to lay dead birds out to cool at the end of the day so they are in good condition for the game dealer to collect.

We then need to get the birds out of the sacks as soon as possible to prevent them heating up, as pigeons will go off more quickly than any game bird. On a hot, muggy day they can start to deteriorate while heaped together in a sack. If in doubt it is easy to check. Just tear off the rump feathers and the skin should look a healthy pinky brown, but it will look green if the bird has started to decompose and is then unfit to eat. This is rare if birds are in sacks for only a short time (never use plastic bags as these cannot breathe or dissipate the body heat of the dead birds). Therefore it is important to get the sacks out of the vehicle and empty them onto the floor of shed, garage or wherever they are to be left overnight to cool – obviously this should be an outside building without heating. Then we will lay them out on their backs. In this way the air can get to them while they lie on a cool floor. If they are to be frozen in the feather this can be done the following morning after they have cooled.

This is the time to select from the bag birds which you need for the table. In late summer and autumn the young birds are easily distinguished and the largest will be delicious in any form of pigeon recipe – Gina and I love them simply roasted. At other times of year it is difficult to age birds, although the young will continue to have a brown tinge to the upper wing feathers for several months after they have got their white neck rings at the time of their six-week moult.

Other birds may be given to friends, and those remaining sold to a butcher or game dealer. If the latter, then a phone call that evening is important to ensure he collects as soon as it is convenient for him. Maybe you have to deliver yourself to the game dealer or butcher, in which case make a plan to do so next day. The important thing, ethically, is to ensure the birds go into the food chain one way or another and make a good meal for someone.

We will bring the guns in to clean and put the battery from the rotary on charge so it is ready for another day.

If we have not seen the farmer on the way home I will phone to report on the day. Remember it is his crop we are protecting, so he will be interested to hear how many pigeons we shot – dead birds do not come back again to eat any more of his crops. Equally, he has given us permission to shoot on his land and so it is important to thank him. A bottle of his favourite tipple to celebrate a good day is rarely refused as a token of your appreciation.

Finally, it is time for that cup of tea and, if I am not going to drive again on a winter evening, a tot of Scotch with a spoonful of honey in the tea is a favourite way to end a good outing.

I hope you have enjoyed your day out and perhaps picked up a few tips along the way.

CHAPTER 9
FLIGHT LINE SHOOTING

Going out to feed

Sometimes, when out on reconnaissance, you will find a strong flight line over the farm where you have permission to shoot, but see that the pigeons are not feeding there. Obviously, if you can follow the line further and find the field where the birds *are* feeding you may have a chance of getting permission to decoy there. However, sometimes that is not possible and so the best option is to shoot the birds on the flight line over the ground where you have permission.

Watch the birds to identify the hedge or belt of trees where the flight line is most concentrated and presents an opportunity to build a hide or stand in the trees to shoot birds as they fly overhead. This can produce quality sport as good as driven game shooting.

The clever thing is to set out decoys where they can be seen by the birds on the flight line. Often they will be happy to investigate and so the flight line can become a decoying day as a bonus. The most exciting situation is when one has the best of both worlds with a variety of shots at those birds passing overhead and the ones coming in to the decoys.

The wind will play an important part in the success or failure of the day. Usually the flight line will be upwind but if there is little strength to the breeze the birds will be passing over too high to shoot. Therefore one needs, ideally, to pick a windy day when the birds will fly lower and so be comfortably within shot. This is equally true for trying to tempt any of those passing birds to respond to the decoys. They are unlikely to do so if flying over way up in the sky.

This is an opportunist form of pigeon shooting but can be rewarding.

FLIGHT LINE SHOOTING

Returning to roost after feeding

The other type of flight line shooting involves ambushing those birds coming back and heading for their roosting woods. These woods may be some miles away and not on the patch you have permission to shoot, or they may be part of a pheasant shoot and thus out of bounds until the season has ended. However, again, there can be an opportunity to shoot pigeons flighting home in an afternoon some distance away from the roosting woods. It is well worth getting to know of these flight lines as often they will be used regularly when the wind is in a certain direction and of sufficient strength to keep the birds low enough to be in range.

You will not make as big a bag as when decoying on a field where pigeons are feeding, but a flight line can produce wonderful sport. So keep your eyes open and learn the regular routes that pigeons fly. They use these like motorways as the easiest routes to or from their feeding destination.

CHAPTER 10
AN EVENING ROOST SHOOTING TOGETHER

We can enjoy very good sport on a late winter's afternoon as pigeons that have been out feeding since daybreak return to the woods to roost. On the many estates and farms where there is pheasant shooting you will not be allowed near the woods until the beginning of February, after the end of the game season. Then the roost shooting is often a perk for the beaters and pickers-up who have helped on the shoot throughout the season. The keeper will allocate a wood to each person, or maybe two or three Guns to a larger wood. In this way, by covering each area of potential roosting woods, the birds are kept on the move, generating more sport as they fly from one to another. It is a form of sport that can produce a lot of shooting but result in comparatively few birds in the bag. The shooting is testing and often Guns get carried away with optimism and start firing at birds beyond the range at which they can be killed. In Churchillian speak: 'Seldom has such a great number of shots accounted for so few.'

However, you and I will go to a favourite wood of mine where pigeons like to roost. Numbers vary depending on the food in the locality but there are usually enough to make a visit worthwhile. One must, of course, pick the right evening, with a south-westerly wind, as this brings the birds in along a

Roost Shooting

AN EVENING ROOST SHOOTING TOGETHER

narrow neck of woodland which concentrates the line as pigeons make for the larger wood behind. Over the years I have, from experience, found my favourite spot. This afternoon the wind is perfect so let us consider what kit we need to take.

Kit for roost shooting

Unlike decoying we need a minimal amount of equipment. This is fortunate, as usually it is necessary to walk through the wood to the position where you want to wait for the pigeons. Therefore, apart from gun and cartridges, I normally take a game bag with my ear muffs and a sack in the hope that we will need it to carry our birds back to the vehicle at the end. A face mask can be a good idea for this form of pigeon shooting because of the angle at which you are looking up and the bird is looking down as it passes over the tree tops. This means your pale face in winter will easily be seen and will cause the birds to jink off and away on the wind before a shot has even been fired. A light camo screen face mask does help prevent this.

Also for roost shooting I often use lofting poles, as a decoy on the uppermost branches will draw birds to your area of the wood. You may use a light seat or shooting stick, but it is best to stand to shoot because the many angles at which shots have to be taken mean that footwork is important.

Finding the best place in a wood

If you have shot a wood regularly over a number of years you will have found the best spot for the various wind directions. However, if visiting a wood for the first time it is sensible to arrive early and take time walking about to see if there is an area with pigeon droppings and feathers on the ground to indicate that it is a favoured area to roost. Pigeon droppings appear as white and brown splashes on the undergrowth, soil or dead branches. These are more visible in dry weather; when it's wet the rain soon washes away these valuable clues.

Then work your way to the downwind side of the wood as the pigeons will approach upwind from that direction. Still assuming you have not shot in this wood before and therefore do not know where the main flight line may be, it is sensible to stand back from the downwind edge at a spot where you can see both sides of the wood. In this position you can load your gun and wait for early arrivals, watching how and where they pass over the wood.

You may get a shot or two but be ready to be mobile and move to the position that best covers the line of incoming birds. Sometimes this is obvious but on other occasions it is frustratingly difficult to assess as there is no real pattern to the flight of birds arriving home to roost.

The time to arrive

We have arrived in our wood on an evening in February at about 3 p.m. knowing it will be dark at 5 p.m. The main flight will be in the last hour of daylight and so we will be patient for an hour, hoping for a shot or two at the early birds coming home. However, there are occasions when the birds may drift back to a wood all day and sport could be at any time. Also, if there is a very strong wind pigeons will start to return to roost earlier and so it can pay to get into position at 2 p.m. to make a full afternoon of it.

Picking a spot to optimise your shots

In this wood I have found a good position which covers the line of approaching birds well. There is an old overgrown pond that creates a hole in the trees which tends to channel the birds and, at one end, I can shoot through the open gap between the trees. This gives a wider arc of fire but means I need to hide well behind this elder bush. So once you are on the line of pigeons look for a place in the wood where you

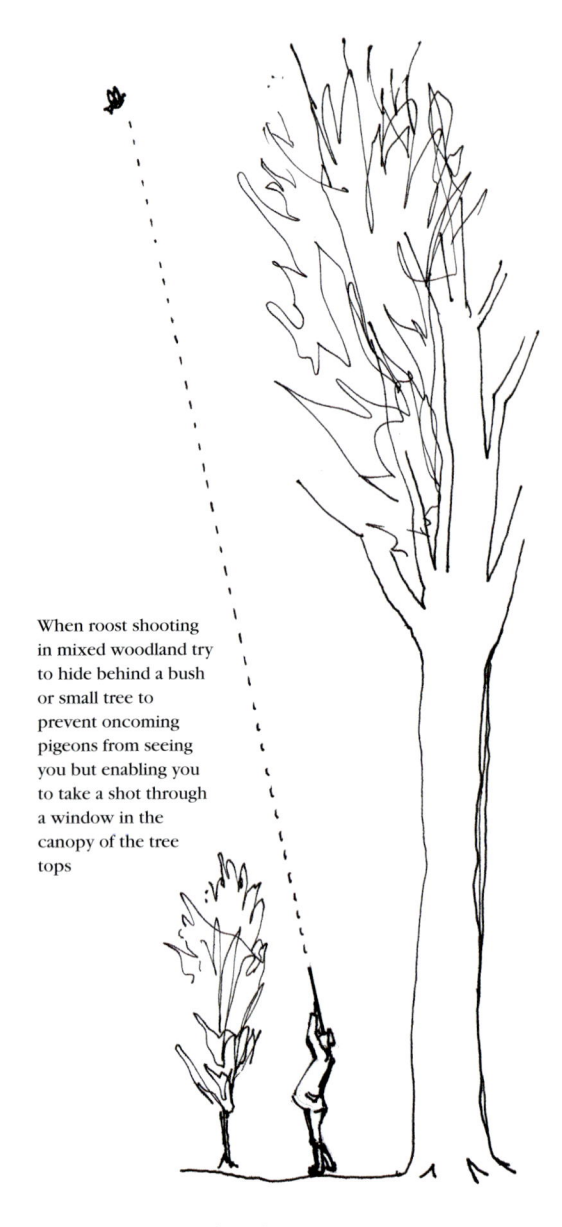

When roost shooting in mixed woodland try to hide behind a bush or small tree to prevent oncoming pigeons from seeing you but enabling you to take a shot through a window in the canopy of the tree tops

Figure 13. *Roost shooting.*

can shoot comfortably through gaps or a window in the canopy of branches. Unless the branches are very dense you can disregard them and have confidence that the shot will go through and kill the bird as cleanly as if it were in the open sky.

If there is a glade or open area in the wood then stand behind a tall bush – look for one at least twelve to fifteen feet high to cover you at the angle at which the pigeon will be looking down (see Figure 13).

On some evenings pigeons will arrive steadily upwind on a repeated line, offering similar shots as they pass a gap through which you shoot. On other days they have no pattern and arrive side-slipping across the wind, or curling to make very testing sport.

Setting up lofting poles

Here we have an oak tree which, in the past, has proved to be a good tree in which to set up my lofted decoy. You want to select a tree with enough branches all the way up to support the poles and prevent them falling sideways. On the other hand, if the crown is too dense it is difficult to get the decoy on its cradle through the twigs and even more tricky to lower it at the end of the afternoon when the light is fading.

Most sets of lofting poles only include four, each about six feet long. These are all right in a hedgerow but not adequate in normal woodland. Therefore I have twelve six-foot poles (they are pre-metric) to extend seventy-two feet up a tree. These are more difficult to handle but they do get my single dead bird, wired onto its cradle, up to the top of most trees. A further tip is that if the wings are broken and allowed to hang free they will lift and rise when the decoy is angled into the wind on its branch. This movement will be an added attraction to incoming pigeons as the decoy appears to be just landing.

On some occasions a lofted decoy will definitely work and bring more pigeons within shot. On other days it is totally ignored.

Taking a shot

Now we just wait, watching generally downwind, for birds to arrive. We will take it in turn to take shots and you can shoot first while I watch from behind you. A group of two or three pass wide to our right, out of shot. Then one comes but lands teasingly on a tree eighty yards ahead of us. Now here is one that looks more promising as it flies positively on a line towards us. Yes, here it comes. You move too early, the pigeon sees you and immediately jinks away the moment before you fire and will live to tell the tale.

So you must wait, keeping very still, having angled your feet to the gap in the trees you anticipate the birds to cross. Also, having seen the bird approaching, you need to raise your gun to address that area of sky where there may be the chance of a shot. So feet, body and gun are in position as soon as you see a bird coming over the trees ahead, but then hold still until the moment of truth when the shot can be taken with the minimum of movement so as not to alarm the pigeon. The gun only needs the final lift to the shoulder as it comes onto and moves through the bird and the shot is fired, all in one steady action.

Let me see if I can demonstrate with the next opportunity. Yes, here are two birds coming and the left-hand one looks as if it will come over our position. I have already moved my feet in anticipation of a shot. The pigeon continues on its line. It comes over the top of the tree in front and into the gap. With barely a change in my body position, which is already at the correct angle, the shot only requires a final movement of the gun, up-on-through-bang. The bird falters, dead in the air, never having been aware of me. Just a puff of feathers drifting away on the wind as the bird crashes down through the branches to land on the dead oak leaves covering the ground.

Now it is your turn again. The bird comes on. You move correctly into position to address it but it passes too far to our left. The next group of four must come. Yes, and you achieved the timing perfectly, with a good shot as a result. The fact that the group exploded up and away, having heard the first shot, made your attempted second shot and the chance of a right and left very difficult.

Rights and lefts when roost shooting are not easy because of the restricted chance of shots through the branches as birds zip away on the wind, frightened by the first shot. So do not be over-optimistic and make sure of your first shot rather than expecting a chance of two. One can be testing enough.

Retrieving shot birds

Roost shooting can be good training to teach a young dog to be steady and only to move on command. Unlike decoying, when it is best to pick up at the end, when roost shooting it makes sense to pick up as you go along, as it will be nearly dark when you pack up.

My retriever, Scott, now knows all about the job. He will wait where told

AN EVENING ROOST SHOOTING TOGETHER

to sit, hidden under a branch or tree, just watching the sky for oncoming pigeons as I do. Then, when one is shot, he will mark it down and, like a coiled spring, will wait for the command to retrieve it. Sometimes if it is nearby I will do so by hand and on other occasions I will wait until there are two or three dead birds on the ground. This means that Scott does not expect to be sent every time a bird falls, as this can lead to a dog running in. By keeping him in suspense he learns to wait for the command and direction of the hand signal for the particular pigeon I want him to pick. Obviously he is sent for a wounded bird immediately. So dog training and efficient picking-up of the birds shot go hand in hand and, by the time the end of the flight comes, there is a pile of dead birds ready to be popped into the sack. Sometimes there may be only a handful, but this form of pigeon shooting can be such good sport on a winter's evening.

You have been getting on well and we have several dead birds in a pile at our feet. We have both had some special shots as well as forgettable misses. It is not easy shooting, so be thrilled at those birds you kill, not annoyed by those you miss. Like all shooting days each is different and so it is when roost shooting. Some evenings the wind will drop and pigeons come over way out of range, but on other days a gale will blow and birds jink about trying to battle against it. In theory the pigeons are flying slowly into such a wind but, believe me, it does not make them easier to shoot as they cannot hold a line and slip left or right, even if appearing to hover overhead.

Now that you have got the hang of it I will leave you to shoot this position and will go across to our left where other pigeons are passing. Between us we will continue to enjoy the variety of shots roost shooting produces.

I hear some shots from you and see birds fall. I get one or two myself and as dusk falls a lone carrion crow makes a mistake, flies over and pays the ultimate price. That deed may save a few pheasant nests from having their eggs preyed upon in the spring.

The end of the flight

Usually there is a moment when the light begins to fade and the pheasants in the wood start to 'cock up' as they go to roost. This is the time to pack up and collect the lofting poles, pick up cartridge cases (if not done after each shot), and assess the bag. Scott has retrieved the last dead bird and now we can see what is in the crops of those we have shot. Oilseed rape leaves are the most common and the birds' crops can be full to bursting. It is important to break open and empty the crops as rape leaves will taint the meat. Even if you wait until the following morning you will find the contents of a crop will smell very strong and nasty as the green matter soon starts to decay.

Other likely contents of a woodpigeon's crop in winter can be acorns, beech mast, spring corn or beans if drilling has started in your area. An ever-increasing winter foodstuff is ivy berries. These are available even in the hardest of weather when food on the ground may be covered with snow. Pigeons seem to love them and will continue eating them late into the spring, when many other sources of food are available.

Having de-cropped the birds we will pop them in the sack and, when loaded up, will retrace our steps back to our vehicle.

When home we will lay the birds out to cool off overnight as, even though it is winter, the body heat of birds confined in a sack will be enough for the meat to go off.

Well, a good evening's sport and another enjoyable outing shooting pigeons that cannot be taken away from us.

We have been decoying, flight shooting and now roost shooting and enjoyed the wonderful sport that the wild and wily woodpigeon can produce. We have helped protect the farmer's crops while having good shooting, and have produced excellent food.

There is nothing more to say but to wish you success: enjoy your pigeon shooting and at all times be safe and respect the people and wildlife around you in the countryside.

It is important to empty a pigeon's crop – especially of rape, which will taint the meat if not removed.

CHAPTER 11
FAVOURITE PIGEON RECIPES

Pigeon pointers

- Woodpigeon is best eaten fresh, not hung to mature as is usual for game birds.
- It is important to empty the crops as soon as possible, particularly after roost shooting, when their crops may be full.
- Pigeon is delicious. Cook what you bag! It is important to use this good meat, so cook it yourself, give it to friends, or sell to a butcher or a game dealer.
- You can select the best of the young pigeons in the autumn, or the fattest at any time of the year.

First, a few tips on how to prepare pigeons for the cook.

Plucking a pigeon

The woodpigeon must be the easiest bird to pluck. It has a strong skin which does not tear and feathers that are removed with ease in handfuls. Nevertheless, here are a few pointers to help make it easy if you have not tried to prepare a bird in the feather before.

1. With the back of the bird held in your left hand, and the head pointing down into a bin or box into which you are putting the feathers, remove the breast feathers up to the neck. Pluck the bird systematically so that each part of it is totally clear of feathers, showing clean skin.
2. Turn the bird round so the tail is pointing down and pluck the lower

front of the bird. Take the tail feathers out in one handful. Then tidy the remaining feathers around the vent and legs.
3. Turn the bird over and repeat the exercise, plucking the back of the bird.
4. Do not bother with the wings. They have virtually no meat on them but to pluck them will double the time it takes to do the rest of the bird.

So far, then, you will have the body of the bird bare of feathers and just head, upper neck and wings still feathered. With a little practice it is not difficult to pluck a bird like this in only a minute.

Cleaning the bird

1. With the bird on a board or worktop and the head pointing away from you, break one leg at the joint. Then nick the back with a sharp knife and pull the lower leg and foot away, which will draw out the tendons of the upper leg. Repeat on the second leg.
2. With the bird still in the same position, cut the 'left' wing off (this is the bird's right wing) at the shoulder close to the body of the bird.
3. Move the body anticlockwise by 90° so the head is pointing left on the worktop. Cut the neck bone at the base of the neck where it comes from the body. Then slide the knife inside the skin along the neck towards the head for about an inch. Pull the neck from where it was severed back towards the head away from the skin of the neck and then cut through the skin well away from the body. This has the result of removing the neck bone but leaving ample skin to cover the front of the bird. If the pigeon has not been previously emptied it will still be intact.
4. Move the body another 90° which will bring the remaining wing round to your left and this can then be removed at the shoulder.
5. Make a slit in the body cavity from below the point of the breastbone to the vent.
6. Peel the neck skin back over the membrane which contains any remaining contents of the crop and remove.
7. Having placed an old newspaper on the worktop to receive the gut, push your forefinger into the body cavity and pull out the gut. Then repeat to remove the heart, which is the organ furthest from the vent and at the

FAVOURITE PIGEON RECIPES

top of the chest. The liver and other internal organs will have usually been removed with the gut.

8. It is debateable as to whether the body of the bird should then be just wiped with a cloth or kitchen towel or run under the cold tap to wash. Personally I do the latter, rinsing out the empty body cavity and tweaking any feathers that may be still on the body.
9. Either put into a freezer bag and seal, or in the fridge ready for cooking fresh.

The whole thing sounds much more complicated than it really is in practice.

Breasting out a pigeon

There are two ways of doing this.

1. To produce the two sides of breast meat still on the bone known as a shield. To do this, lay the bird on its back and part the breast feathers between finger and thumb of left hand. Take a sharp knife and cut just the skin down the centre of the breastbone. Then, with both hands, ease the breast skin, still covered with feathers, away from the centre, then work out and back, revealing the full breast meat of both sides. Then press your thumb under the point of the breastbone and lift upwards. The whole shield will come away from the carcass until it is just attached by the shoulders either side. Insert the knife to free the shield with breast meat complete on the breastbone.
2. To simply remove the breast meat, do as in the first stage of 1. above, i.e. with the bird on its back, cut the skin down the centre of the breastbone. Then, without needing to peel back the skin, just make a cut with a very sharp knife (a fish filleting knife is ideal) down either side of the keel of the breastbone. Then, using the knife close to the bone below each side of breast meat, gently ease the meat from each side away from the skin before severing from the shoulder. Ideally the meat has been cut close enough to the bone to include the tender pale-coloured inner muscle.

Remove any yellow skin tissue remaining on each succulent piece of breast meat ready for the pan or pot.

This operation has been achieved without even plucking a feather and the total skin, feathers and bones of the bird are discarded in one piece.

Either put in the fridge, or into freezer bags in a batch suitable for one meal or two. Allow two or three breasts per person.

Recipes

The secret of cooking pigeon is to cook young ones at a high heat very quickly and older ones at a lower heat very slowly for two hours or more. This longer cooking could be done the day before you eat it.

My wife Gina is an excellent cook and has, over the years, perfected her own special pigeon recipes. We also enjoy those created by our great friend Prue Coats who, as Archie's wife often had pigeon on the menu. Prue is well known for her masterful and delightful country cookery books, and many thanks are owed her for permission to include her recipes for wokked pigeon, pigeon breast stuffed with cream cheese and garlic and breast of pigeon goodwife. Her recipes and a selection of Gina's follow. Most of these recipes are easy – I hope you enjoy them.

Roast young pigeon

Ingredients

1 whole plucked young pigeon and 2 rashers of smoked bacon per person
1 small onion cut in wedges
A few tablespoonfuls of red wine
Your usual gravy ingredients
Redcurrant or cranberry jelly and potato crisps to serve

Method

Put bacon over breast of pigeons, place in roasting pan and surround with onion wedges flat side down. Cook at 200° C/400° F/Mark 6.

After fifteen minutes remove the bacon and keep it warm, to allow the breasts to brown. After another ten minutes check to see how cooked the birds are. Remove from the hot oven while the pigeon meat is still pink inside and not quite cooked as much as you want it. Put them in a warm place to rest and they will still go on cooking a little. It is safe and delicious to eat them when the meat is just a little pink inside.

Add wine to the pan and stir and scrape up the caramelised bits and make into gravy. Serve whole and eat with steak knives or cut the breasts off and arrange on the plates with the bacon and onion. Redcurrant or cranberry jelly and crisps are good with pigeon.

Wokked pigeon

Serves three or four

Ingredients

8 pigeon breasts (4 pigeons)
Unsalted butter or salted butter and oil for frying
110g/4oz brown mushrooms, finely sliced
2 cloves of garlic, finely chopped
1-2 tablespoons redcurrant jelly
2 tablespoons mustard
3 or 4 shakes of soy sauce
3 or 4 shakes of Lea & Perrins Worcestershire sauce
Pepper
Salt if needed
150ml/¼ pint single cream or half cream and half Greek yoghurt (not fat free or half fat, which will split when cooked)
To serve, rice or pasta or buttered toast and salad, ready before you fry the pigeons

Method

Cut the pigeon breasts into four thin strips lengthways. In a large frying pan or wok, heat the butter until foaming and throw in the pigeon strips and cook for only a few seconds, stirring furiously. Add the mushrooms and garlic and fry quickly for a few seconds more.

Add the redcurrant jelly and get it to melt. Then add mustard, soy sauce, Worcestershire sauce and pepper. Add the cream and scrape all the nice brown bits off the pan up into it. Bring up to the bubble. Serve immediately or it will get overcooked.

Sleight of hand, dexterity and speed are of the essence as the pigeon strips should still be faintly pink inside.

Pigeon breast stuffed with cream cheese and garlic

Ingredients

2-3 breasts of young pigeon (1-1½ pigeons) per person
1 teaspoon cream cheese with garlic and herbs per breast
2 eggs beaten up in 2 tablespoons of milk
Plain flour with salt and pepper
Breadcrumbs, preferably fresh not toasted, homemade in processor
Unsalted butter, or salted butter plus oil for frying

Method

Insert a sharp knife along one side of each of the breasts and make as big a pocket as possible. Take a teaspoon of cheese and insert with a rounded knife, spreading evenly.

Put the flour, the egg and milk mixture and the breadcrumbs in three separate cereal bowls. Dip each breast into the flour, then into egg and milk mixture and then coat with crumbs. (This could be prepared ahead and put in the fridge for a few hours.)

Heat the butter until hot in a heavy based frying pan. Cook the pigeon breasts for no more than three minutes on each side. They should be faintly pink and tender. If cooked any longer they will be like rubber. The cheese can get very hot.

Pigeon burgers

Serves four to six

Ingredients

12 pigeon breasts (6 pigeons)
6 herby sausages, skinned
4 teaspoons mustard
4 teaspoons Worcestershire sauce
Lots of herbs, preferably fresh chopped e.g. parsley and thyme (or dried mixed herbs)

FAVOURITE PIGEON RECIPES

Pepper
Juice of 1 lemon and stock (if serving with vegetables) or burger buns, sauces and salad

Method

Cut each pigeon breast into four pieces and put them and the sausages in a processor. Chop briefly in short bursts, keeping the meat coarsely chopped.

Add mustard, Worcestershire sauce, herbs and pepper. Turn processor on and off briefly just to mix. Shape into twelve burgers about an inch thick.

Fry only four at a time, in a very hot pan until brown on both sides and nearly cooked through, but bouncy when pressed.

Now complete the cooking one of two ways, making sure that the burgers are not pink in the middle because sausage must be cooked thoroughly.

For serving with vegetables, after frying the last burger, add the juice of a lemon. Stir between the burgers to get the caramelised bits into the juices. Add a few tablespoonfuls of stock, cover the pan and simmer for a few minutes to complete the cooking.

Or, for serving in a bun, continue to cook a little longer without adding the lemon and stock.

Pigeon meatballs and pasta

Serves four to six

Ingredients

Pigeon burgers as in previous recipe, made smaller
Tomato pasta sauce
Pasta
Grated cheese

Method

Make up the burger mixture into smaller flattened balls and fry until cooked through. Pour tomato pasta sauce over the meatballs and bring to simmer.
Serve with pasta and cheese.

Breast of pigeon goodwife with mango chutney

Serves four

Ingredients

12 pigeon breasts (6 pigeons)
2 large onions, in thick slices
110g/4oz butter
4 tablespoons mango chutney
1 tablespoon Worcestershire sauce
A stock cube
A little water
Salt and pepper
Cornflour to thicken if needed

Method

Brown the onions slowly in half the butter, lift out and put in a casserole.

Lightly fry the pigeon breasts in the rest of the butter just to seal the juices in – less than 1 minute on each side. Lay them on top of the onions.

Crumble the stock cube over and spoon over the chutney and Worcestershire sauce. Add a few tablespoons of water to prevent sticking. Bring to simmer, cover tightly and cook at 150° C/300° F/Mark 2 for two hours or more until tender. Check now and then to see if more water is needed to stop drying out.

When cooked, thicken the sauce if liked with cornflour mixed in a little water.

Serve with rice and poppadom crisps or with mashed potato.

FAVOURITE PIGEON RECIPES

Pigeon and steak casserole

Serves four

Ingredients

8 breasts, quartered (4 pigeons)
450g/1lb braising steak in cubes
110g/4oz streaky bacon in the piece, or lardons
25g/1oz butter
450g/1lb smallest onions
220g/8oz small mushrooms
25g/1oz flour
600 ml/1pint stock
150 ml/¼ pint red wine
1 garlic clove, chopped
Fresh herbs, chopped

Method

Cut the bacon into small cubes. Quarter the onions, leaving enough of the root end to hold together. Cut the mushrooms into halves or quarters according to size.

Fry the bacon gently in butter in a pan until lightly coloured, lift out and put in a casserole and keep warm. In the same fat gently brown the onion quarters and garlic, being careful not to break them up; remove to the casserole. Then, fry the mushrooms. Then quickly fry the pigeon breasts and steak, to seal and brown, in batches so they don't stew. Remove to the casserole.

Add the flour to the butter in the pan and cook, stirring continuously until pale brown. Add the wine and stir and then the stock and herbs. Bring to the boil and pour over the meat and vegetables in the casserole. Put on the lid and cook gently, never more than simmering, preferably in the oven at 150° C/300° F/Mark 2 for about two hours or more until the meat is tender. Serve with vegetables. Serve also with warmed unsweetened croissants sliced in half horizontally if you want a quick pie effect.

Pigeon and steak pie

Serves four to six

Ingredients

The contents of the Pigeon and Steak Casserole cooked as per previous recipe
Frozen puff pastry or short pastry, thawed

Method

Put all the cooked meat and vegetables from the casserole into a 1 litre pie dish with a pie funnel or upturned egg cup in the centre. Spoon over enough of the sauce to come only to the top of the meat and save any extra to serve with the pie. Allow to cool.

Pigeon and Steak Pie

    Roll out the pastry, dampen the flat edge of the pie dish, lay a strip of pastry all round and dampen the strip. Then cover the filling and the strip with the main piece of pastry. Press down on the edges and trim and shape them. Cut a small hole in the centre of the top for the steam to escape.
    Bake at 200° C/400° F/Mark 6 about thirty-five minutes or until the pastry is golden and cooked through and the filling is very hot.

CHAPTER 12
STORIES OF MEMORABLE DAYS

What does a perfect day's decoying looks like?

Many pigeon shooters dream of the perfect day's decoying. It doesn't happen often as there are so many reasons why things can go wrong: the weather; agricultural activity; pigeons moving on to the neighbouring farm, or just not interested in your field, despite it being blue with feeding birds the day before. There are a thousand problems waiting to test you. We can dream of the perfect day however, and there can be no better venue than a field of spring drilling. There is something very special about this freshly cultivated soil where the seed is drilled into the fine tilth. Whether barley, wheat, beans or peas, all can attract enthusiastic feeding pigeons.

So imagine the chosen field of the day which, following a telephone call from a farmer friend, led you to check it out the previous day and you saw pigeons coming on several flight lines to circle before spiralling down to join their mates. As you arrive to shoot there are already a number of birds on the ground, which is encouraging, and indicates that there is enough spilt grain on top for another good feed. The wind is in a perfect direction to shoot from a thick hedge with a single ash tree which will be a focus for arriving birds. A hide is easily created with poles and camouflaged netting and clumps of ivy. Handfuls of tussocky dead grass complete the hide, from which you can have a good arc of fire, yet will be well hidden from approaching birds.

The forecast is good, with a breeze strong enough to give birds a direction to approach upwind to your pattern of decoys, which show up so well, each bird glowing silver grey in the sunlight on the newly drilled soil. Broken clouds scud across the blue sky; it's a day pigeons will fly a good distance for food. No sooner are you comfortably settled in the hide than the first bird approaches without hesitation to swoop into your pattern of decoys. Gun up – bang! – and a single shot leaves a few feathers to drift away on the wind like snowflakes, the dead bird now becoming a part of the decoying pattern.

The birds start to arrive on the flight lines you had observed the previous day. They too are convinced that your decoys are their mates already feeding at the corn restaurant, as they turn to float on the wind as they approach. A right and left boosts your confidence. More dead birds are added to the flock of decoys, creating ever-greater encouragement for the new arrivals to the field. Some birds are dropping in from a great height. They circle before closing their wings to stall and, like darts, they descend from the blue.

The bag is growing and there are still a few hours of feeding time left. You are pleased you brought extra cartridges. Then there is a lull and a chance to find the coffee flask and sandwiches – the discovery of an extra chocolate bar from your wife is a pleasant surprise. Then the sport picks up again and shooting is exciting as, in the last hour, pigeons return to the field to get a crop full of corn before returning to their roosting woods.

A call comes in from the farmer on your mobile to ask how things are going. 'Wonderful', you say. He says he'll come and help you pick up. It's also okay for you to drive round the headland to load up at the end of the day. And what a day – not a record but as good as it gets nevertheless – dream on.

When a good neighbour becomes a good shooting friend

Pigeon shooters are rather like cock pheasants: we both have our territories. The difference is that ours are made up of the farms over which we shoot. I have developed a friendship with a chap who shoots in the area south of me, realising that at times we can help each other.

STORIES OF MEMORABLE DAYS

My neighbour is a great character but too modest to allow me to call him by name. He is remarkable in that he only has one leg and supports himself on crutches. The passion and enthusiasm he has for pigeon shooting overcomes any thought of disability in all that is involved. He reminds me so much of my mentor, the legendary Archie Coats. Coincidentally, my neighbour has the same initials as Archie, so I'll refer to him as AC.

We met on a farm track at 10.30 a.m. AC explained the layout of three adjoining pea fields. A few birds were already landing in the middle of the largest, while others flapped out of woodland onto the edge of the field furthest away. AC's reason for asking me to join him that day was that, while he could shoot from a hide in the hedge of that far field, he could not possibly get out into the middle of the largest one. I set off with all of my kit on my back or slung around my neck to struggle out into the centre of my prairie of peas.

No sooner had I loaded my gun than the first birds arrived and swooped into the decoys with great confidence. Others followed and obviously these pigeons had not been shot or disturbed on this field before as they decoyed like days of old. Nowadays pigeons are usually so 'decoy shy' that they only make a difficult passing shot, but on this occasion the shooting was not as testing as usual. Within an hour I had forty on the clicker.

Sadly I was not hearing many shots from AC's field. We were in contact throughout the day on the walkie-talkies and he told me that there were only a few birds visiting his decoys, but he thought it would improve as the afternoon went on. For me the two lines of pigeons coming to my field flew as if on rails straight to the spot I'd chosen. By 4 p.m. my century was up but I could do nothing to help AC. There was no way he could join me, as walking with crutches through two-foot high peas just cannot be done. He decided to move to intercept a flight line back to the big wood. This was fairly successful but not great. AC repeatedly said that at least he was keeping them off his field.

Still the pigeons came on and I was having one of those dream days when birds seemed trained to drop to shot. The double century was scored by 6 p.m. for an economical 217 shots. I was then on cloud nine after a finale of another sixty-eight birds with only two misses. However, I'm not kidding myself, the statistics illustrate that it was one of those rare days when pigeons were suicidal and produced comparatively easy shots.

We were packing up by 7 p.m. Luckily Ian, the farmer, a giant of a man, helped carry sacks of pigeons back to the car. AC, propped on his crutches, stood watching on the track, laughing and saying it was my fault we had to carry such a load off the field.

I had a can of beer for each of us to enjoy and put the world to rights. Everybody ended the day happy, AC and the farmer because the peas had been protected and me with the joy of that job. My conscience was eased a week later when AC shot a good bag on a field of mine that I asked him to shoot while I was away on holiday. So, territorial respect and co-operation can work successfully.

Big birthday, big shoot, big trouble

Yes it was the 'big 60' and a weekend of very happy celebrations with family and a few of my oldest mates. There were kind presents to remind me of my age, of items that had worn out after years of good service – like cartridge belt, game bag and shooting coat.

I had a great day's partridge shooting on the day itself in Norfolk but decided a day out decoying pigeons would just complete the celebrations. I had been watching several fields of wheat stubble which, having been subsoiled, had rekindled the interest of a good number of pigeons. It is a difficult area to shoot, being on the outskirts of Cambridge and criss-crossed with footpaths, cycle ways, the main rail line to London and with urbanisation on two sides.

On the day it was clear that the fields nearest the town were of most interest and there was a belt of trees which ended in the middle of three stubbles. This would be the place to best cover the situation. The problem was that the wind was a fairly strong south-easterly and if I set up with my back to it my shooting would disturb the community. So I shot with the wind in my face to shoot away from the houses and hopefully smother the sound of my shots. Therefore it was all wrong according to the classic decoying scenario. It started slowly with a few passing shots and I went out from the hide to set up the first ten dead birds. I then had birds start to come out from the suburbs on a line from my left. Some came over the trees and others skewed awkwardly into the decoys as the wind prevented a frontal approach.

Shooting started at 10.15 a.m. and after only once coming out of the hide the sport just got better and better until I had a hundred by 11.50 a.m. As the wind strengthened it became clear that the birds could not place the sound of the shots and they came in, or over, from all directions. I was having every type of shot in the book as they approached high from my left or like downwind grouse from my right. I had never had such fast action and in the next hour I had another 128 on my clicker and then a similar number in the next hour – over 250 between 11.50 a.m. and 1.50 p.m., which works out at one every twenty-eight seconds. I had taken out two cases of Gamebore clear pigeon cartridges, many more than I have ever fired in a day before, but I realised I was going to run out. I phoned the farm office but the owner was out and the farm manager had no access to cartridges.

I had 390 on the clicker at about 2.30 p.m. when, from the north, the police helicopter appeared. It often does if there is a man on the run, or traffic problems. However it then hovered for a few minutes before starting a wide circle. Actually it did a great job of moving pigeons off two other fields and I kept shooting, but I then had the realisation that I was the centre of its ever-decreasing circles. I was within waving distance to the lookout officer.

Still pigeons came and I was now over the 400 and the chaps looking down would have seen me in the middle of an acre of grey bodies.

'Hello there, hello there – police approaching', was the cry I then heard from behind. Out of the trees came a policeman and not just a sergeant, an officer, with a lot of shiny bits all over him. He turned out to be the Cambridge Constabulary Chief Inspector. Was I a criminal? No – I was a law-abiding member of the community pigeon shooting – so I had no reason to feel guilty. I stood up and made a show of unloading my gun before putting it down. From my car they had checked my name with the licensing authorities. Actually it was all very friendly and after a brief assessment of me and my purpose there, the helicopter was told to stand down. I showed a photocopy of my shotgun certificate which I always carry in case of just such a drama. This had already been checked with the firearms department. In fact the Chief Inspector used to enjoy a bit of pigeon shooting himself and was more interested in my sport than the problem. However some well-meaning member of the public had reported a World War Two sound of battle and the police chose to respond purposely. Aerial surveillance was backed up by the local school being put under curfew, with nobody allowed out of the buildings until the ground patrol had assessed the situation. Having clearly seen that I had considered safety and made efforts to minimise disturbance we chatted for nearly half an hour. I suggested that the officers could watch if they removed their yellow vests, which did not complement my camouflaged position. However they decided to go and I shot out the last of my two boxes of cartridges by 3.15 p.m. with 437 on my counter. I then took two hours picking up but could not gather birds from the gardens the other side of the field, or the belt of trees along the main road where several had collapsed. However, I picked over 90 per cent. What an exciting birthday with by far my record day. Maybe there's still life in the old dog yet – if I stay out of prison.

I later contacted the Chief Inspector to discuss a policy to avoid a similar incident in the future. It was agreed that it was impractical for pigeon shooters to notify the police whenever they were in action, although people lamping foxes at night are recommended to do so. However, I have arranged that I will telephone when I am to shoot in that sensitive area in the future, or near other residential areas. We countrymen with legally held shotguns are living in an evermore sensitive era created by criminals or lunatics with illegal firearms. Sadly those fields will never produce a good day's sport again. As I write a new road and a thousand houses are being built there. The fields may have gone but nobody can take away that memory.

When pigeons fly north

Do pigeons migrate? This is a much debated and little researched question over which there is great controversy. I believe the answer is some do and many do not. There is always a resident population in an area, the density of which will depend on the balance of feed, roosting and nesting habitat throughout the year.

However, at the end of the summer there will be flocks of young birds which will need to move to find adequate winter food, whether this be rape or southern England's woodland harvest of acorns and beech mast. Conversely, in the spring, there is a movement north following spring drilling which starts in the south in late January and can go on until late May in parts of Scotland. It is not a global migration that takes place but, in Britain, a national movement of mainly birds of the year.

With the advent of winter rape since the 1970s, and in more recent times it being grown further and further north in Scotland, it is probable that fewer pigeons now need to move south in winter. The resident population is now much greater than in the past, when winters were harder and a meagre living on turnip tops was all that was available.

I was migrating north myself in the third week of May to work on painting commissions on the rivers of Sutherland where few woodpigeons ever venture in summer, let alone winter. I had been invited to visit a mutual pigeon fanatic in Aberdeenshire, Andy Hill. We first met on the BASC woodpigeon working group, on which he represented Scotland. Our rendezvous on this occasion was at his handsome stone-built house up in the hills above Deeside.

We would cover some interesting and very beautiful pigeon country in Andy's Land Rover. Wide open valleys of mixed farms, with small fields which

STORIES OF MEMORABLE DAYS

gave way to hill farms and heather-topped uplands and grouse moors. Some valleys were sparsely wooded but other areas were forested. The glens were rich with mature hardwoods which had only just broken into leaf.

In the afternoon we visited an area where two large fields, each of about seventy acres, had been drilled with barley two weeks earlier. A haze of two-inch green blades rose and fell across the rolling fields of this big bowl of ground. The exciting thing about it all was that there were perhaps four to five hundred pigeons spread evenly across these two fields feeding enthusiastically.

Andy knows his area and covers in the region of a hundred farms. With the poor April weather in the north, the pigeons had arrived late from the south. It was interesting that, on the subject of pigeon movement, seen from his end of the telescope in the north, we were therefore in total agreement – maybe we are both wrong but here we were looking at pigeons which were not here a week ago. He had not fired a shot on the farm this spring and, on inspecting the fields, we could see that the attraction was partly undersown grass seed as well as the ungerminated barley on the surface which had not been gleaned soon after drilling – which obviously meant that there were no pigeons there earlier.

So next day we arrived at 10.30 a.m. to look again and sure enough, even at that time, there was activity and odd pigeons and small groups arriving from two main lines. It looked good but Andy was apprehensive that it might dry up by midday. We decided to set up and see, and to shoot from two hides almost on the diagonal corners of the large square-shaped area. We would both have a crosswind as it turned out, as the wind backed to become better for both of us as the day progressed.

I was soon in action and it was fast and furious. In fact by the time Andy was set up an hour later, and first called up on the radio, I'd shot fifty. The pigeons worked in a big circle when he started shooting and the day became fairly even for us both. The day brightened into the most ideal conditions, clear sky with broken cloud, sometimes a brief shower and all with a fresh westerly wind. I could see Andy's decoys with the naked eye even though we were about threequarters of a mile apart. The light was so clear and pigeons showed up well on the soft green crop. Certainly the pigeons could see them, as at times groups came in at a great height over the grouse moors to Andy's left and just folded their wings. At other times he said they came like snipe through the whins below the heather line. This was because a peregrine was playing and doing feint stoops on these passing pigeons and making them very skittish.

I had shot a crow early in the day and set it up to the right of my decoy pattern. Another came and I did likewise. I ended up shooting twenty-four carrions and two hoodies by the end of the day, which was a record for me. The secret was that I was in a very good hide on the edge of a black conifer strip and in shade when the sun was out.

Andy pointed out that the farming here is really as England was in the 1960s, but with the additions of a few fields of winter rape. As was suggested earlier this is the reason for more resident winter pigeon in Scotland. I found I had much in common with Andy in terms of approach, belief and techniques of decoying, although he did surprise me with his maxim of the 'three Ss' for pigeon. The first two are probably self-explanatory – Seed and Safety – but Andy feels that the flock offers the same opportunities for wild times as clubbing and pubbing, hence Sex! His pigeons north of the border do seem oversexed according to his stories of them trying to mount his decoys and floaters, or gang-raping a bird on the ground. My Cambridgeshire southern pigeons lead a very sober and puritanical life compared with all the rape and pillage of the North!

Average days for his clients produce bags of thirty to forty birds so our day of 393 head, including crows, was exceptional. But, Andy pointed out, as we had only fired 508 shots between us, our score rate was high. On our return Andy's cheerful partner Kitty greeted us, late though we were, with a marvellous meal. As we collapsed into armchairs afterwards with glass in hand, we had to agree that these pigeons had migrated from the south; fact not fiction.

Halcyon days

Few things in life give as much pleasure as when a son enjoys his father's sport. Some years ago it was therefore a wonderful day for me to sit in a hide watching my son Henry shooting pigeons on a field drilled with barley. Henry was then of an age when one would have assumed that he had been shooting pigeons for ten years or more. Certainly I remember his first shots, taken with a .410, as clearly as I'm sure he does. However his young life of school, university and then working in London has not produced as many opportunities to go pigeon shooting as we would have liked. Nevertheless, he has developed into a competent shot at whatever quarry is on the menu.

The previous day we had visited the field in order to observe the flight lines and assess the best position for a hide. Reconnaissance is always important and in this case I wanted to check that the pigeons had not found another drilled field nearby. Some had, but the main activity was still on the original field and, provided the wind remained the same, one or two skimpy thorn bushes would provide the basis for a hide. It looked promising and we were quite excited as we returned home to prepare our kit and load up the car for the next day. However, I sometimes have to be careful that observation is not superseded by optimism; with pigeons sport is seldom certain.

The next day dawned and the omens were good; a rare dry day was forecast with a moderate north-west wind. Ideal conditions, but it was a cold wind and so we erected the old canvas horse blanket that I have used for years as a back wind shield. Then, while I set up other poles and nets, Henry cut some elder from the hedge at the end of the field. The buds had burst and this haze of young green leaves completed the extended bush, producing a spacious hide for the two of us. The decoys were arranged as a casual feeding group to complete the scene and then I left Henry to carry on as I had to meet someone and would be away for an hour or so.

On my return I could view the situation from a rise on the track. Through binoculars I was encouraged to see many more pigeons set out as decoys than we had started with. A pigeon swooped in from the left, there was a puff of feathers and it dropped dead. I heard the delayed noise of the shot as the sound reached me. I continued to watch as several more singles or small groups decoyed well and, nearly every time, one or sometimes two puffs of feathers heralded more dead birds to join the now impressive display of decoys.

I joined him in the hide and little encouragement was needed, his smile said it all. I had lent him my clicker and he had it hanging from a hide pole. He rose and shot another and clicked the twenty-eighth. I sat enjoying just watching, my arm still in a sling from my hand operation a fortnight earlier. It suddenly felt so much better that I slipped my bandaged hand into a free position and tried three shots myself. Not a tweak of pain and I happily realised I would be back in action earlier than I had anticipated.

It is interesting to watch others pigeon shooting from a hide. Most inexperienced shots tend to jump up too early. If anything Henry could help himself by rising to shoot a little earlier, as some pigeons came within range but drifted away without him being able to shoot. I talked a few of them in, to give him the timing to create the optimum opportunity of a shot. 'One from the left approaching decoys, gently up now, steady, mount, shoot!' He soon learned the benefit of standing up slowly, not to leave it too late and then jump up like a Jack-in-the-box, which alarms the pigeon and makes for a more difficult shot.

Henry explained that he had shot the birds on the left better than those on the right so I suggested that he adjust his seat and feet 45° right of centre. This immediately helped and he was able to kill birds to his right more easily. His previously limited swing to the right was then opened up, creating a wider arc of fire. A good right and left at the next two birds proved the case and reminded me of a very spontaneous and amusing reply he gave when, aged about 4 or 5, I had asked if he knew the story of the two pigeons, to which he replied, 'Yes Daddy – BANG – BANG.' Now my story had been realised in his shooting.

As we ate our sandwiches Henry pointed to the clicker which at that stage read thirty-seven, equalling his previous best bag. The sandwiches went flying as another pigeon appeared from nowhere and obligingly hovered over the decoys while his gun came to hand. With a very focused shot it became a record statistic. Numbers aren't everything but Henry's total when we packed up was fifty-four. He had shot very well and no one can take away that fact. It was a perfect day shared together leaving memories that will live on – several stitches in the rich tapestry of life – and not a little pride as well as pleasure for old Dad.

Boys will be boys

We love seeing enthusiasm for the countryside and the sports we enjoy in youngsters, for it is only through them that these sports will continue in the future. I recently met two young lads who had the enthusiasm and sense of adventure that I remembered so well as a boy myself, free to explore the countryside around my home.

I had received a phone call from a friend who farms south of Cambridge, where part of the land is well inside the city boundary between a council estate and the mainline railway to Liverpool Street. He said that there were a lot of pigeons on a bean stubble, which was soon to be ploughed. 'Would I like to have a go at them?' No difficulty in giving him a spontaneous reply, 'Yes – I can't go tomorrow but will be there on Saturday.'

'Look out for the public footpath on the north side of the field', he said.

I arrived in good time on the Saturday and cut an elder bush from the derelict scrub behind the council allotments. I then dragged it behind the car to the position I felt was the optimum for the strong south-west wind and yet away from the footpath. The field was some 300 yards wide and I was therefore 200 yards from the path and 100 yards from the farm track on the opposite side.

The forecast was for heavy showers driven on the strong wind and so I

STORIES OF MEMORABLE DAYS

made a substantial hide behind me based on an angler's big green umbrella. My son Henry was possibly able to come later and so I used poles and nets to make a spacious hide. This was completed with the elder branches, so creating an enormous new bush in the open stubble.

Pigeons soon started to come and my shots disturbed others on fields downwind, which came on a line up to me. This was going to work unless conditions changed. One can never take anything for granted with pigeons. However it was not the pigeons coming to the field that surprised me but the number of people, not just on the footpath but also walking the farm tracks. By mid-morning I was in the middle of a continual circus of dog walkers, joggers, mountain bikers, horse riders and mothers pushing prams. Saturday, I soon realised, was not the ideal day for me to shoot this field! However the pigeons kept coming. Amazingly very few people seemed to either notice the new bush in the landscape or hear the shots on the wind. I had to set the decoy pattern to create shooting down the length of the field so my shot did not land anywhere near the footpath, but I also had to keep a sharp eye as to where people were.

About midday the pigeons suddenly started turning away and not coming in to the decoys. I puzzled for a while and then decided to perhaps alter the pattern. As I came out of the hide I saw three young teenagers standing only twenty yards behind, two wearing white T-shirts and the third bright orange! 'Hello boys, how can I help', I said. 'Oh, we've just come to watch', they replied. I explained with surprising calm and patience that while they stood there in bright clothes there would be nothing to watch. I suggested they withdraw and watch from the burnt-out car on the sugar beet pad at the end of the field. A few empty cartridges in their pockets and off they went, watched for a quarter of an hour, got bored and disappeared back in the direction of the council houses.

An hour later the pigeons again turned away. This time I stood up to look over the angler's brolly behind me and sure enough there were two more boys standing there. 'Please mister, we've just come to watch'. I again explained the problem to these two youngsters and that I was in a hide made of camouflaged netting and taking every precaution not to be seen in order to fool the wary woodpigeons. 'Ah yes', they said, and off they went with more empty cartridges provided they did not tell any other mates. It had been a meeting with the first boys which had encouraged the intrepid second party of lads.

Three-quarters of an hour later, excited voices behind me warned me to again look behind. There were the two youngsters now dressed head to toe in camo gear. 'After what you said mister, we went home and changed, are we all right to watch now?' Well, what could I say but respond to such initiative and enthusiasm and welcome them into the hide.

Mathew and Leroy, aged 8 and 9 respectively were like two excited puppies. I had them stand behind me under the umbrella, peering out through the netting for the coming pigeons. I explained what I was doing and they soon had their sharp little eyes competing to tell me of incoming birds. I told them to put their fingers in their ears when I put the gun up to shoot, to protect their hearing. They referred to my hide as a 'den' and soon entered into the spirit of excitement and sport. I explained how one could tell by the result of the shot whether the bird was hit head, tail, right in the pattern or just winged. They loved it with morbid delight. 'That's dead all over', was Mathew's cry when a pigeon had flown into the full choke pattern.

Conversation with these two was no problem and they were very much at home in the suburban countryside. I was honoured to be invited to see a dead fox they visited every day in a roadside ditch. It had obviously been hit by a car. I declined as politely as I could such a prestigious invitation to the hallowed shrine of the month-old dead fox. My score by now, about 4 p.m., was 174 on the clicker round my neck. To keep them amused when not smothering Conon, my golden retriever with fuss, we played mental arithmetic games of how many I needed to shoot to get 200. Eight and nine-year-olds have lots of fingers and thumbs, but not enough to solve such a problem. However they soon had a countdown and at 200 we celebrated by sharing my packet of crisps and two remaining sticks of Kit-Kat. All this and still shooting a few latecomers before picking up. I dismantled the 'den' and they started collecting the bag of pigeons together – a slow business with only one pigeon at a time in each hand held by the tail. Two boys counting pigeon into sacks does not work either with chatter, mucking about and forgetting the first number they thought of.

We loaded the car and with a last cuddle for Conon off they went home happily with every pocket bulging with empty cartridge cases. I cannot think what they told their mothers but I know there will be two boys who will not forget the day. In a few years time they may or may not pass GCSE maths, but for sure their enthusiasm will ensure they are countryside supporters.

Neighbourly relations

A phone call from a local farmer friend about pigeons on his spring rape was to spark off something of a challenge. He had seen a flock of a couple of hundred on his two small fields of spring rape in the nearby parish.

STORIES OF MEMORABLE DAYS

I went to investigate next day and yes, sure enough, there were pigeons – actually more than he had suggested – but only then did I see the difficulties involved in trying to shoot them. One field was about six acres behind some houses. The second field was even smaller, only four-and-a-half acres. It was square with one side adjacent to the road and a house on three of its corners. Therefore both fields had two similar problems – first, there was no safe arc of fire into either field from any side and second, disturbance to the occupants of the houses could be socially difficult. Am I getting more sensitive in my mature years, or is it the increasingly delicate political issue of shooting? Probably a little of both, but the crop was certainly being destroyed in such small fields. I decided to shoot on the Monday to minimise disturbance to those in the village snoozing in their gardens on a Sunday afternoon.

Plan A was to put plastic bags on the six acres adjacent to the eight or ten houses to keep off pigeons and hopefully bring them onto the smaller field where I proposed to shoot. I then visited the three adjoining houses and was pleasantly surprised that the chap on the western corner was all for the pigeons being shot to save his vegetables. The little old lady on the north side was equally enthusiastic and urged me to shoot the pheasants too! I explained that was not my remit, nor legal at the end of May. Nobody was home at the third house on the southern corner, so I popped a note through the letterbox. So much for local PR and I felt better now that I had support rather than aggro from at least two out of three neighbours.

The next problem was how to shoot safely. Luckily, there was a south-westerly breeze, which meant I could make a hide under the old oak in the field. It was easy to make a good hide so that my decoys were between me and the eastern corner. The boundary of the field was only thirty-five yards away so any bird between me and the ash tree on that edge was well within range. I could then shoot safely over open fields with the sound of my shots taken on the wind away from the houses and village.

So it was about 2 p.m. when I set up and immediately had one or two customers. I started with just a dozen static decoys but the new dead birds were added to the picture. The other advantage of angling my shots as I did was that the shooting disturbed any pigeons that had come to the six acres and trees around it. They immediately flew to my field, not being able to place the bang which had put them on the wing. This meant that when one or two produced shots I would nearly always get another shot within a minute. I had to be very careful to keep strictly to my limited arc of safe fire so as not to drop shot anywhere near the houses. This gave only a narrow angle of about 45°. On so many occasions I could have shot birds on my left or right but had to refrain. However, the sport was not just steady but brisk, with most birds coming as singles.

The shooting was not particularly difficult as they either decoyed well or made satisfying crossing shots flying along the tree tops at a known thirty-five or forty yards. In such a cosy corner it was possible to shoot very consistently and things were going well. So well in fact that after two hours there were one hundred on my clicker. I had originally thought of taking just a bag of cartridges, hoping for forty or maybe fifty birds, but luckily I had taken a case of 250 instead.

There was a lull at about half-past four but an hour later, with a sunny evening, sport picked up again. The main line came from over my right shoulder, passing downwind between me and the field boundary ash tree. Rather than wait for them to pass and maybe turn upwind they made better sport on their first downwind pass. It also meant that those following just saw the leader collapse among the decoys and so they came on and in many cases did the same!

Tim, the farmer, came to watch from the road for a while as he heard the steady shooting from the farm. By 6.30 p.m. there was another hundred on the clicker and I was running short of cartridges and half an hour later the last shot fired to end play on 221. Luckily it was a very good moment for Tim to reappear and as he approached his eyes widened – he saw the bad news that half the field was grazed flat by pigeons and the good news that it was covered by a carpet of grey bodies. Crop protection and good sport makes great friends of farmers and pigeon shooters.

We picked most but I was reluctant to let Conon hunt the hedge too much for the last few outlying birds while game was nesting. Such a good day is rare but never had I shot a bag like that on such a small field. Before driving home I revisited the three neighbours to offer them birds from the day's sport and Nature's own bounty.

Pigeon perfect

I spent an enjoyable day in a pigeon hide with arguably the world's best shot and current holder of the pigeon shooting record – George Digweed.

It was with some apprehension that I had looked forward to this. It was rather like being on the front row of the grid next to a Formula 1 Champion or partnering Djokovic at tennis.

George had just returned from South Africa as FITASC World Champion for the third time, whilst I'd arrived home chuffed to bits with a bottle of port won at the CLA stand at the Game Fair.

So here we were, as guests of Phil Beasley, dropped on a rape stubble and left to get on with it, whilst he took two American clients elsewhere. Actually I felt it was with his customary sense of humour that he'd lit the blue touch paper of an explosive double firework and stood back out of danger! The blue in George's big bang were his Digweed Royal Blues, a 35g cartridge loaded by Kent Cartridge Company, having been developed for long range performance. The blue in Phil's case was his colourful language!

George shot with his 32-inch barrelled Kemen choked full and full. I had my Spanish side-by-side, 28-inch barrels bored ¼ and ¾ and used Gamebore 30g 'Clear Pigeon'.

We watched the field, actually two adjacent fields with a hedge between and both agreed on the way we read the situation from pigeons we saw feeding and flying about. We decided to shoot from the middle hedge but about a hundred yards from the belt of trees at the far end. Our cars were used strategically to prevent pigeons settling at the other end of the two fields. These, with the noise of shots, would hopefully keep birds moving upwind to us.

Soon we discovered a big difference in approach to hide building. George likes an open-topped 360° visibility hide whilst I prefer one with a tall background and a partial top to the rear half. This prevents birds spotting me if they come from behind before turning into the decoys. He prefers to have full vision and stands all the time whilst I shoot sitting down.

So we built two hides together parted by one camouflage net. We used foliage to soften the effect and set out our fifteen dead birds as decoys. We agreed on this and had them in two groups about twenty yards out from the hide. Incoming pigeons would hopefully come to the gap in front of our hide between the groups. I was surprised that George agreed with the idea of decoys placed comparatively close in, considering the range he can shoot. However, we have the same philosophy – you can always take them further out or make more rights and lefts but if the decoys are far out, you don't have so many options to increase your chances.

Now how would we operate together? Would I even get a shot? It soon became clear that I am happy to take on anything up to fifty yards but that is the sensible limit of my game gun. But George has the skills and power of shot to kill birds out to eighty yards – yes, eighty yards. He suggested that I take anything which came inside my range and he'd take anything, passing, by or over or beyond fifty yards. 'One for the popgun', he'd say as a bird came to the decoys and he left it for me. If two came we did a synchronised

The Lost Bird Retrieved

shooting trick of me taking the left and he the right. When on occasion three or four came then again, a flurry of shots and the sky was clear but for feathers drifting away on the breeze.

The system worked 'perfect' as George said and I was interested to see just how gentlemanly and generous he was. In fact I've seldom found it easier to shoot with anyone sharing a hide. The vital thing, of course is safety and I would always advocate making two adjacent single hides rather than one big one, so each gun has a clearly defined shooting area and angle.

Toby, George's black Labrador, was an experienced campaigner with his nose pressed to the netting at the front of the hide, marking long, winged birds. A gruff 'Go on' from George and Toby was off like a whippet, usually straight to the bird. If he needed redirecting when out, then a whirring of arms, two-fingered whistles and shouts of 'Go back you bugger', or other well chosen phrases, were all registered by Toby as an encouragement to do his own thing. People queue for George's shooting masterclasses but I suspect his dog training classes are less well attended! However, Toby usually found the pigeon and returned exhausted to the hide more for a drink of water than to deliver the bird to hand.

STORIES OF MEMORABLE DAYS

However, what was incredible was George's shooting technique and I can see how he achieved his record bag. It begins with exceptional eyesight as he spots pigeons before they appear as dots on the horizon to a normal eye and he can identify a stock dove from a woodpigeon at a range before most people would first see it was a bird at all. So then he's ready in his open-topped hide. On this particular day they were decoy- and hide-shy so just passed by, giving long rangy shots. However, when within seventy to eighty yards he would shoot the birds with amazing consistency.

I asked him what he focused upon when shooting such birds. Was it lead, speed or line? 'Line is everything', he said, 'Squirt far enough ahead and the shot string will take care of lead – but if it's not on line, there's no chance.' He seemed allergic to birds within fifty yards but, where a normally competent shot finishes, George Digweed starts.

What did surprise me was that he did not wear hearing protection – George, while you can still hear, listen to the good advice and look at all the deaf old codgers you meet. I'd hate you to miss my shout of 'Good shot' if we should enjoy a day together again.

It was not a big day as the lines faded and the pigeons found quieter fields in which to feed. However, the lulls gave us time to chat about the shooting world in general and not just about his top-class clay competitions but also about game shooting, which is really George's great love – not heady numbers days but the quality high birds of the Devon shoots, flighting teal or making a mixed bag on the Romney Marshes.

On normal game shoots he is a victim of his own success and often finds himself in a no-win situation. If he leaves birds he doesn't consider sporting, his host and keeper say how do we give him a shot. If he kills everything, they and fellow Guns say there's nothing left for the rest of the season. If he were to miss, they'd never stop pulling his leg and laughing. Instead of being thrilled to admire and acknowledge a unique shot of world skill, he becomes resented in a cloud of jealousy, notably on the competition circuit. Here is a man who respects his quarry, is a good naturalist, understands the country and shoots with a high standard of ethics. His problem is that he's just too good a shot. He's often driven to think he'd rather be alone in a hedgerow with his dog and the chance of shooting fifteen or twenty pigeons.

In any other country he'd be a national hero and household name but for some reason British world clay pigeon shooting champions are only known by those who venture between the covers of the shooting press. The man's a legend in his own time and I enjoyed sharing the day – while a three-figure bag was not forthcoming, the sixty pigeon picked gave us sport enough and memories which will live on.

Pigeons and the public

A large triangular field of about twenty-five acres had been drilled with peas, and the seeds had gone in so well that, apart from a little on the headlands, none were left on top.

However, a phone call from Jamie the keeper informed me that surprisingly a number of pigeons were on the field one afternoon. I went next day to observe and indeed by 3 p.m. there were more than enough to get me excited.

Overnight I made plans as it was not straightforward. The three sides of the field were surrounded by footpaths. It was Easter Saturday and there could be people about.

It is never easy to set up in the centre of a field and fool pigeons to come near a new feature in the landscape. However, with a net hide surrounded by branches of white thorn flushed with early leaf, the overall appearance was softened. It was 11 a.m. when I had set out my fifteen dead decoys, together with two crows. A similar number of artificial decoys built the flock to what I hoped would be a convincing picture. Although, the previous day, I had noted that the pigeons on the field were focused around the edges where the few peas might be gleaned from the surface, I was relying on the headlands being disturbed by walkers like mobile flankers. In this way, I hoped to turn a negative into a positive but then I have always been an optimist – an essential characteristic of a pigeon shooter.

So the scene was set and indeed it was a pleasant morning. I had all the time in the world to watch the traffic on the motorway beyond the footpath on the southern side, the odd cloud in the sky and a man who took over an hour to walk his dog around the field. By midday I realised I had definitely either started too early or worse, that the pigeons were going elsewhere to feed. By 1 p.m. little had changed with only two shots at birds passing wide.

As occupational therapy, I had a spare clicker counting people who appeared on any of the three paths around the field. Yes, it was that boring but anything helped pass the time. There were twenty-two on the people clicker with only two on the one for pigeons. Then the pigeon traffic picked up in the lunch hour, and so by 2 p.m. the score was thirty-two people to twenty-nine pigeons. Could the pigeons win I wondered, as a party of nine parents and children appeared on bikes? An elderly couple with a dog were going around the field in the opposite direction to a young lady with two doddery old Labradors. However, the pigeons did the desired thing and floated out on a line to me in the centre of the field. Many decoyed surprisingly well, but I had to pick my shots to angle them away from people or the motorway.

My decoys were set so I could shoot towards one corner of the field which was maybe 600 yards away, well out of shot, although the middle of each side of the triangle was half that distance. Whilst perfectly safe, it was important not to frighten or upset anyone. Luckily there was not a problem and few people even looked up when a shot was fired.

A gang of student joggers was followed by two horses with riders. However, although the pigeon traffic was easing down their count was ahead by 3.30 p.m. at 52:49 in favour of the pigeons. Later a line of birds came over high from behind. Some were just in range and made very satisfying shots, others passed wide but a few decided to snack on their way home and took a wide circle into the decoys.

My pattern was now convincing, with maybe sixty fresh birds set up accompanying the original ones. I reached ninety on my clicker and whilst this was double my optimistic hope for the day I hung on for another hour and just made the magic century. The total public count was sixty-six and they had done a great job keeping the pigeons from landing on the edges. I picked up ninety-four (pigeons that is) together with a couple of crows.

In any pigeon shooting book this experience would come in the chapter on advanced decoying and, like some television demonstrations, it should be added that this should not be tried at home.

A good bag

What is the secret to the consistent success of shooting good bags of woodpigeons over decoys? It is a question frequently asked. I recently realised, by counting back in my game diary over the last ten years, that I have averaged over a hundred pigeons a day. I therefore ask myself this same question to see if I can learn from the answers as I must be doing something right. One just does not get lucky that often. To share my thoughts may be of interest.

First, the fact is that I do not always shoot a lot of pigeons and the average of a hundred birds a day is actually made up of days from only two pigeons, to my best day of 508. So I do get it wrong at times but, in retrospect, there is usually a good reason for this. Either the weather defeats me or something happens agriculturally that changes feeding patterns overnight. Some modest bags are on what I call 'duty shoots', protecting a crop at a vulnerable stage when there are not a great number of birds but the few that are feeding are being a real nuisance to the farmers. However, my experience enables me to read a situation reasonably accurately, to the point of estimating a potential bag within 10 or 20% from my reconnaissance, whether it be twenty birds or 200.

I am fortunate to be in a good pigeon area. However, research has shown the density of woodpigeons to be high throughout the grain-growing areas of the British Isles. Yet in predominantly grass and stock country, as found in western Britain, the pigeon population is lower or, at best, patchy.

The big question is therefore, whatever the pigeon density, how do you get yourself in the optimum position for the best sport? I could say there is no easy answer but actually there is: you need to spend a lot of time on reconnaissance. I am fortunate to work for myself as an artist so I can detour on my daily journeys or make purposeful visits to different farms to keep watch on the current situation. Ideally I am one step ahead of the pigeons, watching the fields as the birds build up on them. If there are crops vulnerable to damage I then keep in touch with the farmer. Most of them are very co-operative as they know that when I shoot I will kill a fair few, and dead pigeons do not eat their crops. Bangers scare birds off but they either get brave and return, or eat other crops, so the problem is only postponed, not cured.

Am I a pest controller or sportsman? Definitely the latter. It is the sport of shooting a wild bird that can produce every shot in the book which I find so exciting. However, the by-product of my sport is the important crop protection it achieves. It is the success of this that ensures my welcome on the farms where I enjoy my sport. So a constant link and symbiotic relationship exists between farmer and pigeon shooter for a win-win situation.

The key therefore is to get myself on the right field on the right day and in the right place on that field at the right time of day. Observation will give me all the answers. I do not need to see great flocks of pigeons but I do want to see a steady flow of traffic. Often pigeons will not need to be on a field for long to pick a crop full of food, so there will be a constant coming and going over a number of hours of different birds, rather like people eating at a motorway service station.

Sometimes there are a number of pros and cons for shooting a field from one of several positions. Usually I have a gut reaction early on in my decision-making and, more often than not, I am in the best place. If I make a hide and set up only to find that, when I start shooting, the flight line changes, then I have no hesitation in spending time moving. I would rather be in the right place for two hours than the wrong one for four or five.

Do I have a routine which I stick to every time? Well yes, but routine should not be confused with recipe. The great challenge is that each situation is different and the fieldcraft must vary accordingly. Even during the course of a day, the conditions and corresponding response of the pigeons will usually vary, whether this is caused by wind, rain, sun or farming activities as a field is rolled, sprayed, harvested, etc. As in life, nothing stands still and the world is constantly changing – so must the pigeon shooter. Another advantage of working for myself is that I can, to some extent, shoot a promising field on a day when the weather looks suitable. I always keep in my mind the outlook forecast for the week and particularly note the wind strength and direction.

So … I have arrived on what I have observed to be a shootable field, on the right day and an hour before I can expect the main activity. This may be at dawn, mid-morning or, in the hot weather of mid-summer, it could be late afternoon. I try to give myself the time to shoot for as long as the pigeons dictate. Often a shoot will be for five hours, sometimes for seven, eight or nine. Frequently people say they shot forty in a couple of hours. Well, at twenty an hour it could have been a hundred-bird day if they had been there longer. Often things start slowly and I question whether I've got it wrong. A steady shoot over a long period may not be a hot-spot, but the protracted sport gives you time to savour the moment and all the birds, plants and wildlife with whom you share that special day.

On arrival, the next stage is to set up decoys where pigeons expect to see them and a hide where they do not expect to see me. Whether in a hedge, on woodland edge, or from bushes dragged out into the middle of the field, I like to get to where the pigeons want to feed. It all sounds so obvious but I often see people shooting from a tree or a hedge conveniently close to where they can park their vehicle, rather than slogging out to the far end of the field where pigeons actually want to feed. At times it is hard work carrying kit a long way and hopefully carrying a sack full of birds back again at the end of the day. I do not travel light as I have spent too many hours in uncomfortable hides without a seat or taken half the day to shoot enough pigeons to make my decoy pattern convincing. I weighed myself once with gun, rucksack, decoys, cartridges, nets and all my kit and found that my eleven-and-a-half stone was matched by the total load I carry out. Half a mile across a sticky ploughed field or along tramlines in standing corn on a hot summer's day and I question my strategy. When I carry it all back in two trips, with fifty or sixty birds in a sack each time, I may be exhausted but happily so.

Again I am frequently asked what is my kill per cartridge ratio? I can usually side-step that and say 'Sufficiently effective'. Since a boy, with my first single-barrelled .410 and my lone sorties around the hedgerows of the local farm, I have always recorded the quarry accounted for and the number of shots taken. I still have a morbid statistical streak and know how many cartridges I take out and therefore how many I return home with. Thus each gamebook entry records the truth, good or less good. As this depends not only on my performance on the day, but the quality of the sport, it is the worst averages that actually indicate the best days' shooting. As I shoot I find that I am clicking, on the counter round my neck, about twenty pickable birds per box of cartridges fired. I would not expect to do that in a strong wind or on a high flight line shoot. Some might say I pick my shots and certainly I have developed an eye for the killable moment of truth. I rarely waste cartridges at birds out of range, and that range for my side-by-side, choked ¼ and ¾ has a maximum of about fifty yards. I reckon to take on anything at any angle, speed or height that I see within that range.

There is no escaping the fact that, to shoot good bags of pigeons regularly, one has to shoot quite straight. Simple arithmetic will show how many opportunities one needs to shoot a hundred pigeons based on an individual's cartridge to kill average.

Shooting pigeons is an acquired art and I have seen good game and clay shots defeated by this sporting bird. The fact is, clays and driven game do not radically alter course in flight like woodpigeons do. Pigeons turn, jink, dive, flare and in a moment an easy shot can become an impossible one. Such is the sporting challenge of the bird and the reason why I love and respect it above all other quarry.

Have I said anything new? I doubt it. However there is something new to learn about the art of decoying pigeons on every shoot. I also know I have never had a day, irrespective of the bag, that I have not enjoyed immensely. It is sport that, as Mr Kipling used to say, is 'exceedingly good' – even if you don't have one of his cakes in your lunch box.

Focus on gold

Soon after he won the gold medal in Australia in 2000 I had the pleasure of meeting our British Olympic hero, Richard Faulds. Not only is he an exceptional shot, but also a great ambassador for the sport of shooting, both competition and game. A young man, quiet and modest, whose responsible attitude to shooting and the politics that surround it is an example to shooters and non-shooters alike.

A year later it was therefore the making of a story for future grandchildren to find myself honoured to stand beside the great man at the award ceremony

STORIES OF MEMORABLE DAYS

of the European Side-by-Side Championships, he having won the hammerless class and me the hammer gun class with grandfather's 1877 gun. The fact that he had a score of ninety-two against many competitors and I had seventy-seven against few, puts the event in perspective. For me, a one-off life story; for Richard yet another championship title.

I spoke to Richard afterwards and conversation turned to pigeon shooting, as it does. I asked if he would be amused to come and have a day with me if I could find something of interest. For the Mr Cool, who contained nerves and emotions until the last pair of the Olympic shoot-off, to be so enthusiastic with open-eyed excitement at the prospect of a pigeon shooting trip, took me by surprise. Yes, he loved pigeon shooting and would be there.

It so happened that the following week a large rape field had been harvested and a flight line had developed between it and the cement works' quarry a mile to the east. This is an attraction for pigeons but as to why I am still unsure. It may be water but more likely calcium, as the pigeons can regularly be seen sitting on the chalk spoil heaps.

Along with the birds, which respond to decoys on the surrounding cultivated ground, an extra sporting element can be provided by a prevailing westerly. In these conditions pigeons make both upwind and downwind flight line shooting. That was Plan A. Plan B would be to shoot the large rape stubble itself, which would produce a larger bag but in normal conditions not such interesting shooting – for the Olympic champion I wanted to offer something challenging.

The day dawned, a bright and breezy forecast, but would the wind back towards the south? I drove round on a final reconnaissance early that morning. Even then the birds were moving and the wind was right.

After a quick coffee at home, off we went to the venue only a couple of miles away. Being in good time, we made a detour and stopped at the top of a hill. After a short walk Richard was amazed by the sight of the cement quarry ranging across some hundred acres and more than a hundred feet deep. Through binoculars we could see a few early birds sitting about and others coming and going. We then went to watch the flight line to the rape stubble. The good news was that there were quite a good number of pigeons moving but the bad news was that, as I feared, the wind was backing to the south. This, in effect, was then blowing across the flight line with the result that the pigeons were dispersed over a front of 400–500 yards. To set up and shoot this would not work as we would not cover enough of the fragmented pigeon traffic.

So Plan B came into play. This meant constructing a large double hide in what I had observed to be the key position in the middle of the 105-acre field. This was achieved with poles, nets and a background of elder branches cut and towed into place from the nearby woodland edge. I set up the decoys, in this case also using a pigeon magnet, to draw birds to the area and hopefully give them confidence to approach the new feature in the landscape, our hide.

I then left Richard to shoot while I watched from a distance to see how the pigeons reacted. If they headed for another rape stubble over the hill, then Plan C was for me to go and shoot there to keep them off. In the event things went well and Richard was soon in action with his Beretta auto and Express Supreme 28g 7.5 shot cartridges. This small shot may win him championships but would it be too frail to kill woodpigeons I wondered? With his accuracy and the Beretta's full choke, the puff of feathers I saw drift away on the wind as another pigeon fell dead, sometimes fifty or sixty yards out from the hide, demonstrated that my fears were unfounded.

Having assessed that the situation was working well, the hide was in the right place and only a few birds were interested in the other field, I joined Richard. When sharing a hide, I like to actually build it as two hides so that there is a net between us and each has a clear and safe separate arc of fire. Safety is always paramount in such situations. I had set the hide cross-wind so the birds would mainly come into Richard as they approached upwind from his side. However, the wind became stronger and pigeons came flaring on past us, not decoying but producing even more interesting and testing shots.

We soon settled to a rhythm as it became clear for whom the next shot was possible. He had pigeons passing wide out to his left and was killing some great challenging birds. From my angle on his right I could see over his shoulder as the shot went true from muzzle to target, up to sixty yards out. I had some fast downwind 'grouse shots' as pigeons came round the shoulder of the hill and then saw the decoys. It was a joy sharing; our teamwork was working well and pigeons were dropping dead out of the sky at all angles.

Richard said he thought our shooting must look a pretty picture from the road. The quality of the shooting in the wind egged us on to take birds at all challenging angles, speeds and ranges. The three-shot auto was at times used fully to account for one jinking downwind bird. Some birds came high, responded to the decoys but were spooky about our hide and turned away still high, to drop back on the wind. I assessed each but felt none were on for a shot. However, Richard decided otherwise and took the last bird, killing it cleanly half as far out again as I would have thought shootable.

I asked Richard what training, practice or mental preparation he needed to produce consistent top-class competition performances. Game shots can miss a bird and just swear at the gun, cartridge, or dog and expect another chance in a minute. However for world-class clay shots, it is more like a test batsman at cricket – if you miss, you may well be out.

Focus and concentration are areas in which Richard found great help from a sports psychologist. The method suggested is of help to us all and yet fundamentally simple. Think, worry, dream of whatever between shots but have a physical moment, which for Richard is the click of the gun closing prior to his next shot, and from that moment focus on the target. This minimises wasting energy unconsciously when waiting between shots, but tunes all senses to a peak for the short period it needs to climax. For game shots I suggest this could be the moment of pushing off the safety catch or the time you mentally say 'Yes' to the bird being yours to shoot.

I gave his advice a lot of thought and used it successfully a month later in a foolish bet I had accepted after a few drams late at night. My Anglo-American shooting friend Barry loves a bet and has a mind for nocturnal mental arithmetic exercises – one of the reasons he is so successful in his international engineering company. His £100 bet was that he'd shoot more pigeons than me next day, irrespective of bag, based on his 1.7 for my one shot.

He is a good average 50% man and it was not until next morning when I awoke that the implication dawned. If he fired, say, 170 shots and picked eighty-five pigeons, I had to do better than eighty-five with my 100 shots. All morning he chuckled and jumped up and down with the joyful anticipation of taking £100 off old Will. We drew for hides from the two positions and the pressure was on, but he did not know about Richard's advice and I applied the counselling.

Pigeons decoyed well and I was delighted to get the first ten with ten shots, twenty with twenty, thirty with thirty. This was too good, but each bird that came died. Whether high crows or jinking second birds of a right and left, none could escape the line of concentration or shot. I hoped Andy Hill, with whom we were shooting, would come to pack us up but no, 5 p.m. was the allocated time – forty, forty-seven, -eight, -nine, fifty straight on the dot of 5 p.m. Never before and, I suspect, never again, will I do it but what a lesson in concentration.

Was it the thought of losing £100 or Richard's advice? Whatever, it certainly worked on the right day. I lost three of the seven outlying birds that tottered back to the wood but picked forty-seven. Barry had got what he thought he needed – fifteen birds picked from his thirty shots – but with dismay reluctantly pulled five £20 notes from his back pocket. I cannot think of anything worthy enough on which to spend my prize, though a drink of thanks for Richard will be high on the list.

After the exciting day sharing a hide with Richard we did not have a cartridge kill percentage to write about, but the 216 birds we picked were all from the greatest quality of sport. Maybe the moral of my story with Richard Faulds is that a young dog can teach an old dog new tricks.

Even the bad times are good

It had been a long week and I needed a day off to go pigeon shooting, my favourite way of communing with Nature and putting the world to rights. So I set of to a favourite area, an estate where I have been fortunate to shoot game for years and always so enjoy my days

There were fewer pigeons than normal this February but one good day on a chopped maize strip and another on a field of spring drilling inspired me to go and look round this particular Saturday. The drilling had long finished and the maize strips were bare. However, I can usually squeeze a bag of pigeons from somewhere unusual, or a flight line. Bill, the keeper, said that he had not seen much about and, after an hour of checking out likely places, I had to agree. However, in the distance a few shots could be heard.

I drove round searching the likely sitty woods or belts of trees for indication of things to come, when from midday onwards birds were thinking of feeding. Nothing caught my eye. A handful clattered out of a beech tree along the track but they drifted aimlessly on the wind over the horizon. It was still only mid-morning and, parking on a hill to watch over a long vista, I drew a cup of coffee from the flask. I nibbled on a leathery Kit-Kat bought at a filling station on the way (I had failed to notice the sell-by date which, like the game on the estate, had been six weeks ago). I'm always amused by products that display in bold print; 'best before end' – that too relates to the shooting season – even life itself! Too much philosophy and not enough pigeons seemed to be increasingly obvious.

When I caught up with Bill, who was out ferreting, he told me that the maize strips on the neighbouring estate had only been chopped that week. Obviously this had drawn the pigeons and the boys were getting their turn of some good sport.

It is rare for me to go pigeon shooting purely on spec without a prior recce but the day was a bonus and so my expectations had not been high. It was getting on for 2 p.m. before I saw a hint of any pigeon traffic, let alone a place worth setting up. Then, on the corner of a maize strip that had been chopped weeks ago, I saw a handful of birds feeding and a few more in a clump of trees in a pit at one end. Then another joined them. Other birds were in trees along the woodside at the other end of the strip.

Memories were kindled as I had had an amazing day the previous year on this maize, shooting in a south-westerly wind, ideal for the trees in the pit. However, this wind was a strong easterly, which would not be good for that end, but it could work from the edge of the wood especially as one or two more birds had flown over two particular beech trees on the same line.

I decided to give it a go as there was nothing to excite me elsewhere and only an hour or two left of the pigeon-feeding day. A hide was easily established in a position to give the optimum arc of fire. Decoys and the rotary were set up on the stubble. This was about sixty yards from the nearest edge of the maize strip but, should birds come to the maize, I felt I could draw them to my position on the sporadic flight line over the wood.

The first customer came wide to my right. It showed absolutely no recognition of the decoys but was unlucky enough to pass an opening in the trees and crashed down further back in the wood, making an easy retrieve for Conon.

A few minutes later a pigeon produced a mirror image shot on the left; another suddenly appeared across my front along the wood, making for a spontaneous shot. I was up the left-hand side of it but it collapsed with a broken wing.

Then a lull before an overhead incomer was followed by a downwinder from behind, which must have been sitting in the trees behind me. From my left, one actually decoyed, swooping round low, making a straightforward shot. Later I missed an easy crosser then killed a high one through the trees, which made up for it.

Every shot was so different and after two hours of not-brisk sport, but with a shot every five minutes or so, I had experienced a shoot of extreme variety. There had been a challenge and the great satisfaction was of making something from nothing. It was a modest bag of twenty-three but each had its own story and had produced a most memorable and enjoyable day. Driving home happily, I was reminded of the sportsman's true saying: 'It's not what you go out to get but what you get out of going.'

Decoying over diggers

As when musicians are called back on stage for an encore, so too did a favourite area of farmland, sold for a housing development, produce a final great day's pigeon shooting.

On the southern edge of Cambridge there is a block of land, which is surrounded by houses, a hospital, footpaths and the mainline railway. Despite this it has produced many exciting days sport over the years. In fact it is where I shot my personal best bag of 508. This same area has produced two of my more memorable *Shooting Gazette* stories, including the one where the constabulary's armed response unit surrounded me on suspicion of being responsible for the outbreak of World War Three.

The area earmarked to become the 'green lung' of this conurbation grew a good crop of wheat in 2007, and was then abandoned after harvest. However, next summer volunteer wheat appeared amongst the thistles and weeds, and the farmer was granted permission by the developers to harvest the bonus corn for pheasant feed. So, after all the other local fields had been combined a fresh stubble was created, and a number of ever-optimistic woodpigeons came for their share of the gleanings.

I would not have known about this situation had Andrew, the farm manager, not phoned to ask if I would like some of the corn for my pheasants at a very reasonable cost. A big 'yes' was obviously my answer. I went to see if there were any pigeons on the stubble, and sure enough an encouraging number were coming and going while others flew like buzzing bees, lifting and dropping into the stubble.

However, there were practical and political problems to overcome if there was to be any chance of a day's decoying. First, I needed to ask permission from the developers' representatives, as the land was no longer owned by the farm. Fortunately Andrew arranged this, because, as farm manager, he was in regular contact with the construction company. The second issue was a concern over safety, as the construction of the new road and bridge seemed to involve as many men as extras used in the film *The Bridge Over the River Kwai*. Health and safety conditions are, I'm sure, better in Cambridgeshire, but still I'm sure they did not want No.6 shot rattling on the crane driver's window or patterned on the side of earth-moving trucks.

To minimise any such difficulty I chose to shoot on a Saturday, when at least the orange-jacketed team only worked until midday. With the wind direction it was possible to build a hide about a hundred yards from the new road and shoot across the field away from anyone, while the sound of my shots would keep the downwind end of the field clear of pigeons.

As rain was forecast I built a good hide around my big green angler's umbrella, which I covered with camouflaged nets and foliage. The pigeons decoyed well, having come on a line either from Cambridge or from woodland to the south. They flew around the crane, over the lorries and trucks and set their wings as they approached my decoys. A busy shoot developed and I was reminded of the old days in Hampshire with my mentor Archie Coats.

It had been a very successful summer for nesting woodpigeons and there were many well-grown young birds on the wing. They make delicious eating when simply roasted and served with redcurrant jelly.

My five hours of sport was very exciting, with an even flow allowing me to shoot forty an hour until it tailed off sharply at 3.30 p.m. It took an hour to pack up the hide and pick up. My dog Scott was busy retrieving a dozen from the deep brook behind me while the old man, Conon, collected outliers from the stubble. With my wagon loaded we bumped our way off the field past the towering cranes and lorries. It was indeed a worthy stage for an encore, but now the final curtain has fallen on those favourite fields of mine.

Memories of the great Archie Coats

My passion for pigeon shooting in the 1960s could lead me to only one man, Major Archie Coats. I had first read about him in *Farmers Weekly* when I was a teenager, and later, in my early twenties, I conceived a way to meet the great man himself. Archie, seeing a kindred spirit, kindly took me under his wing, and he and his ever-patient wife, Prue, became friends for life. I spent many happy times at their Hampshire farmhouse, with its low-beamed ceilings, squeaky doors and dogs on chairs in rooms cluttered with family treasures and old pigeon shooting photographs.

As an ex-Scots Guards officer, Archie's orders for the shoot day were explicit, with map references, points of the compass and 'sitty' trees pinpointed as the plan of attack on the grey hoards was explained. We'd chug along in his battered old blue Land Rover, the back full of camouflaged nets, poles, sacks with decoy dead birds and the ancient five-gallon oil drums beaten by the ravages of time which acted as our seats. The front cab would be full of blue smoke from Archie's pipe as he told his stories of the Raj or duck shooting in the reed beds of the Egyptian marshes.

We'd arrive at our destination having travelled miles through Hampshire or Berkshire down narrow country lanes. Like an Edwardian boy's annual, every field we passed was like turning another page on an exciting story of a day shooting pigeons in a gale, fog, blizzard or thunderstorm. Archie knew every bush or tree where, over the years, a hide had been built to outwit the pigeons. The irony was that he actually loved the woodpigeon and, like any true sportsman, had immense respect for this quarry.

Interestingly, he had a somewhat blinkered vision of the countryside. If any plant, insect, crop, bush or tree had ever been eaten, nested or sat in by a pigeon he would know everything about it. And yet, other birds, flowers, bees or butterflies of beauty to senses of sight and sound held little interest to him.

'Think like a pigeon' was his great saying. He did, and even on days known as 'Major disasters' – when the flocks seen on reconnaissance the previous day failed to show – he would chunter on. Never that he had got it wrong, of course, it was always the pigeons who were blamed for not being where they were supposed to!

Archie was a brilliant shot and was modest about his cartridge to kill ratio. He knew to a yard the range of birds he could kill and, if they were within that net, they were rarely missed. Most shots were taken from a sitting position to allow for maximum movement. As a game shot he excelled for two reasons; first he had nimble footwork, and second, as when in a pigeon hide, he was always alert, with intense focus. I was once drawn next to him on a day's partridge shooting and did not see him miss a single bird during a drive. When I congratulated him later he said, 'No, I missed one', – meaning he'd missed an opportunity of one and that moment of inattention was the same to him as a missed shot to any other game shot.

Archie was the founding father of the art of pigeon shooting and a legend indeed. For many years, his 1962 record day of 557 stood unbeaten, and had he not run out of cartridges twice he may have shot a record that would still stand today. Some elements of pigeon shooting have now changed with the efficiency of modern farm machinery and the pressure of so many now enjoying the sport. However, the principles in his classic book, *Pigeon Shooting*, are still the same.

I still feel his presence alongside me in the hide with colourful comments, some of which I don't need like 'bad shot Garfit – more lead' and others that are quite frankly unprintable!

Out in the field with Peter Theobold

While days out game shooting are sociable, and chatting to all involved is an enjoyable part of it, pigeon shooting is more the sport of the loner. It involves reading weather conditions and reconnaissance to create sport for the individual hunter/gatherer while communing with Nature.

So most of my pigeon shooting days are spent alone, testing my wits against this wild and canny bird. I enjoy the planning of a day from previous reconnaissance, which hopefully leads to a strategy to optimise my chances.

STORIES OF MEMORABLE DAYS

Occasionally there is a situation with challenges I like to share, and I have a few pigeon shooting pals who are equally fanatical about the sport. Such a day arose early one summer and Peter Theobold joined me to shoot a seventy-acre field of spring rape.

Peter and I can sometimes enjoy sitting, or watching and talking about how to shoot a field, assessing various options as we pool our experience. We sometimes spend far longer making a plan than actually shooting, but we both agree that two hours in the right location is better than six in the wrong one.

Our day had some interesting challenges. The large, rectangular field had a rise of ground across the middle. There was a wood at the far end from the road where we entered the field. Belts of mature woodland stretched the length of the two long sides joining the wood to the roadside. From the day the field was drilled the farmer had positioned two gas guns banging into the centre of it. For weeks no pigeon thought of settling on the field and if it did then the farmer soon disturbed it during his routine patrols.

However, when the crop was about four inches tall, one of the gas guns broke down. The other was then moved to the centre of the field. The pigeons eventually became braver and began to feed at each end away from the gas gun. In fact, they did not move even when the three delayed bangs disturbed the peace every fifteen minutes.

Peter and I arrived at about 12.30 p.m. I explained the situation and, having observed it previously, was able to suggest the spot for him to build a hide out in the field at the road end where most of the birds had been seen regularly feeding. The obvious place would have been from the tree belt on that side, where birds had also been dropping in, but the trees overhung the field and decoys would not have shown up as well as in the open. Also, any pigeon that did come to a hide on the edge of the woodland would probably fly to the trees, disappearing behind the canopy before a shot was possible. Pigeons from behind would over-fly the decoys altogether.

I set up at the other end of the field in a hide also in the open between the game strip beside the wood and the rape. This was not a key feeding area, but would hopefully produce shots at birds flying near the wood. I estimated Peter would get 130 and I could get around the seventy mark. Maybe this was brave and, if true, would certainly be a big day.

Peter was soon in action and with constant conversation on the radio we monitored the day even though the hill prevented us from seeing each other. His birds decoyed well and although my end produced fewer chances, high passing shots made for great quality. With little wind we both needed to spin around on our swivel seats to take the birds at any angle in the hide.

All continued well and we had clicked a hundred by 4 p.m. in the proportions predicted. Then my end suddenly improved and we both enjoyed great sport until we packed up three-and-a-half hours later, with Peter accounting for 151 birds to my 120 – considerably more than anticipated. What a great day for two pals and one made very sociable by the chat and constant monitoring of events aided by modern technology.

Just don't shoot the combine

On a farm a few miles from home there was a field of laid barley. I had just arrived in Norfolk for two weeks holiday when I received a phone call from Nigel about great numbers of pigeons feeding on the soft green grains. I explained that I was away for a fortnight and would have to pass. On my return I phoned and Nigel said that the birds had left the area, but he added that I should come over and have a look around if I wanted to.

I did call in and met Brian, Nigel's father, who confirmed there were only a few local birds about now as he drove round each afternoon, honking his horn to get them off the eighty-acre field. However, I observed enough pigeon movement to make me feel it was worth a try the following day.

On arrival there was little activity, but over the half hour that followed a trickle of birds seemed to favour flighting to one area of the woodland belt along the western side. Having set up, the first customers decoyed well, then a few more over the next hour. It was nothing record-breaking but good sport.

The heavy drone from a big engine back at the farm broke the relative tranquillity of the field – surely not a combine harvester? A minute later Brian's white truck came into view and he came to tell me they had decided the barley was fit for harvest. Not good news to the lone pigeon shooter having good sport.

Sure enough the monster red combine appeared at the far end of the field and started the first bout around the headlands. However, after no more than a hundred yards it came to a halt. In the distance I could see men peering at the inner workings with body language that emitted question marks. After a false start or two the diagnosis was obviously not good. All went quiet and the men returned to the farm. However, Nigel wandered along as he had watched as pigeons had continued to fly around and those that decoyed or flew within range were addressed with shots from my Beesley.

Nigel is a natural sportsman and serious cricketer, but also a keen shot so crept into the ditch behind me to watch. He explained the problem with the combine and said the mechanic from the local agent was on his way to fix

STORIES OF MEMORABLE DAYS

it. In the meantime Nigel wanted to watch and we enjoyed a chat while he waited.

Now I would not want you to think that I wished ill health on the combine harvester which would potentially end or at least spoil my sport, but certainly the breakdown was good news for me. Pigeons were now coming from all angles across the big field and shooting them was very exciting.

At about 4 p.m. the cloud of dust and drone of the machine indicated the harvest show was back on the road. Nigel was corn-carting with his tractor and trailer and the inevitable was creeping ever closer. It took the combine harvester about three-quarters of an hour to crawl around the large field and eventually it came past me at point-blank range. I was engulfed by the roar of the engine, whirring blades, belts, auger and straw processors, leaving me in a cloud of dust and barley husks.

Not only was straw being defecated by the machine, but puffs of grey feathers punctuated its journey past me as shot birds were processed – not oven-ready but plucked and minced. Other birds which had fallen through the barley were pickable in the stubble but too many of them had inevitably been squashed by the wide tyres.

The pigeons kept coming however and seemed little concerned. The good news was that as the machine went around the far end of the field it disturbed any pigeons that had tried to feed there. They lifted and flew upwind to my position. So the combine had a positive function as flanker or beater aiding my exciting shoot.

Each circuit of the field meant I had to move my decoys and rotary to avoid the same fate as those shot birds hidden in the corn as the machine passed – but the pigeons kept coming. Eventually it was time to pack up, having waited for the late arrivals to just reach the double century. What I was lucky to do on his barley field Nigel may well have done on the cricket field the following weekend.

Conon and Scott found picking up confusing as they arrived with the odd wing or a flattened chapati-type pigeon. Others were retrieved from under the straw rows.

My record day

My personal record day was on a field of wheat grown for seed trials and, when completed, there were small blocks unharvested but not required. In October these were flailed off and so several tons of wheat was scattered on the stubble. It did not take long for all the pigeons in the area to find this easy food source just as their normal stubbles or drillings had ended. It was a field of only about twenty acres but difficult to shoot. Being situated on the edge of Cambridge there were footpaths on two sides and a small roadway for cycles and foot traffic on a third. The fourth side had the mainline railway to London. I therefore had to erect a hide in the middle of the rectangular field so that I could shoot down the length of it towards the railway line, which was well beyond the range of my shot. However, the two public paths either side were within range of dropping shot and so I was limited to my safe arc of fire.

My hide in the centre of the field was surrounded with branches of elder bushes from nearby woodland. Luckily the wind, being westerly, was perfect and I started shooting at about 11.30 a.m. Pigeons came from the moment I was in my hide and I was soon busy as they decoyed well. Even with my limited angle of fire, I was amazed to find I had a hundred birds down in the first hour. Such fast action is very rare and, although I have done that before, it only lasts for a short time. However, things continued as they had begun and there were 200 on the clicker after two hours and 300 after three.

There were four good lines of pigeons coming to the field and rarely was there not a bird or two coming on one line or another. The gun barrels were hot and I was glad to have a handguard on my old 1907 Beesley side-by-side. Still birds came on and they must have been flighting from a great distance as they continued to decoy well. I kept having to leave the hide to bring in the dead birds which fell way out beyond my decoys, as they attracted the incoming pigeons to come only to the limit of range.

It was not until 4.30 p.m., after five hours, that the pigeons stopped coming. The prospect of picking up such a large bag was going to be exhausting in itself but Jamie, the then new young keeper on the estate, kindly arrived to help. We bagged up the sacks, each containing fifty dead birds. Just over 500 were picked and he then took a photograph for posterity. The Addenbrooke's Hospital was in the background beyond the railway line. It is now history and as I write 800 new houses are being built as Cambridge ripples out. So, this being my personal best bag ever was a bonus and I wonder who will live in the house which was the site of that memorable hide.

APPENDIX 1
PIGEON SHOOTING AND GENERAL LICENCES

There is still some uncertainty about the legal basis for pigeon shooting today. This section is intended to remove many of the doubts and questions.

Why general licences?
In 1990 the UK government was threatened with the European Court for not having a close season for the woodpigeon (among other so-called 'pest' species) as required under the EU's Birds Directive 1979. This could have resulted in a nine-month close season since the woodpigeon can nest through so much of the year. Government, farming, shooting and other organisations worked hard together and persuaded the European Commission that the woodpigeon is such a serious problem for farmers and horticulturalists in the UK for much of the year (being virtually non-migratory) that year-round measures were needed to protect crops. General licences proved the most acceptable means of formalising the continued shooting of pigeons for crop protection.

What are general licences?
There is no single 'open general licence' as many shooters seem to think. Each year the statutory agencies (Natural England, Countryside Council for Wales, Scottish Natural Heritage and Northern Ireland Environment Agency) issue specific general licences to authorise management of various wildlife problems or issues that otherwise would be illegal under each country's main conservation legislation. They are 'general' and 'open' licences in that there is no need for an individual pigeon shooter to apply for a particular licence.

Currently each country has two or three general licences which include woodpigeon – for preventing serious damage (typically to crops) or disease, preserving public health or safety (air safety) and (in Northern Ireland), for protecting wild birds. Each licence allows the killing of woodpigeons for its stated purpose and under specific terms and conditions, by 'authorised persons'. Be aware that terms and conditions vary from country to country and between different licences. In Scotland, for example, the relevant licence must have been read before any shooting is carried out. In Wales, air safety and protection of wild birds are also covered. Ignorance of the law is no defence.

An 'authorised person' is basically the owner or occupier of the land in question or somebody authorised by its owner or occupier, by a local authority or other statutory agency.

Each general licence sets out clearly what can and cannot be done by the licence 'holder' while carrying out the licensed activity. This is why, while it is not a requirement to have a copy of the relevant licence when out pigeon shooting, it is highly advisable to know precisely what the licence allows and prohibits.

A key requirement under such a general licence is that its user 'must be satisfied that legal (including non-lethal) methods of resolving the problem are ineffective or impracticable'. This does not require each pigeon shooter to test and assess other pigeon-scaring methods before shooting pigeons over crops. It also does not mean an end to roost shooting or shooting away from vulnerable crops, including over stubbles. Similarly, the pigeon shooter does not have to prove pigeons are actually causing damage before shooting. In effect the UK government and European Commission accept that crop protection needs are broadly met by shooting pigeons over or in the general vicinity of arable land where pigeons are likely to cause problems on different crops and at different stages of crop growth.

Other key points

The essence of the legal requirement when shooting under an appropriate general licence is to make it clear, if challenged by a duly-authorised person (e.g. policeman), that the shooting complies fully with the licence's terms and conditions. Any failure to comply fully may lead to prosecution. Giving 'for sport' or 'because it's a pest' as reasons for the shooting may well result in a court appearance.

The types and terms and conditions of the various general licences in place in each UK country can be found on the websites of each statutory agency (NE, CCW, SNH and NIEA) as well as on the BASC's website.

Notable terms and conditions include the legitimate use of unrestricted semi-automatic shotguns, which are prohibited for shooting wildfowl and game birds. Another condition is that birds 'must be killed in a quick and humane manner'. The licences recognise that some wounding of birds inadvertently occurs but require all reasonable effort be made to minimise wounding and suffering of shot birds. The woodpigeon may be agriculture's number one bird pest but it is still a sentient creature and should be afforded the same respect as any other bird (or animal) subject to sporting shooting or pest control. The image of shooting is not enhanced if pigeons are carelessly shot and not properly retrieved and, where necessary, humanely dispatched.

General licences are renewed annually after being reviewed by the statutory agencies. There is not always consultation with the organisations who may be affected, so changes may not be well publicised. In order to keep within the law, therefore, it is wise to check the appropriate website(s) around the turn of each year to be aware of any relevant changes affecting use of the licences.

Be aware that shooting pigeons in back gardens is difficult to justify under a general licence's terms and conditions, and several shooters have found themselves in court as a result.

While pigeons make for great sporting shooting, technically we should not refer to them as 'quarry'. Defra advised some years back that true 'quarry' species are those which have an open season and are protected the rest of the year. The woodpigeon does not have an open season under the general licence system and so does not 'enjoy' quarry status.

Other pigeon species are often encountered by shooters, including feral pigeon (not strictly a species) and collared dove. These too are covered by general licences, and the same rules and advice for shooting apply to them. However, the stock dove is fully protected in most of the UK, although it appears on one Scottish general licence to protect air safety.

Feelings can run high on general licences, but to seek their withdrawal, or jeopardise the current system by bad practice in the field, is not wise. Under the EU Birds Directive the alternative to our system would be a close season, and possibly a very long one from March to November. Farmers, horticulturalists and shooters really would not want that.

Finally ... in light of the above and possible uncertainties over pigeon shooting under a general licence, it is better to play safe, and, if in doubt, ask before setting out.

John Harradine
1 December 2011

APPENDIX 2
WOODPIGEON SHOOTING – HOW DOES SCIENCE HELP US DO IT BETTER?

Thanks to the farmer's need to protect his crops from damage, pigeon shooting is widely available and hugely popular. It can provide excellent sporting shooting and a very tasty meal at the end of the day. So, what is the best gun and cartridge combination? A simple question but the answer is less easy. Many pigeon shooters have their own preferences for a day over decoys, pigeon flighting or, after the game season, roost shooting. Others will ask their gun shop or follow guidance in the sporting press and shooting books.

In 2003 the BASC asked more than a hundred pigeon shooters what cartridge(s) they used. Not surprisingly, perhaps, 32g of No.6 proved the favourite, followed by 28g or 30g, also No.6. More recently, a membership-wide survey revealed that some 40% of pigeon shooters used 28g, nearly 30% used 30g and 24% used 32g. Three-quarters of the sample – nearly 1,100 – used No.6 shot, with 10% using No.7 or 7½ and 8% using No.5. These findings suggest a shift towards lower cartridge weight, while still using No.6 shot.

So, this is what many pigeon shooters are using. But, wearing my science hat that, of course, does not necessarily mean it is the best to use!

Let use try to define a starting point. The first consideration surely is the ethical one – what gun/cartridge combination is best able to achieve a consistently high kill rate, and wound or lose as few birds as possible? This should be the objective of all responsible shooters. To avoid wounding and loss means less suffering of shot, but un-retrieved, birds and low wastage of good meat. The woodpigeon may be agriculture's number one bird pest but it is still a sentient creature and should be afforded the same respect as any other species. Whatever the pressure to clear a crop of pigeons, they should never be left flapping. Bear in mind also that others may be watching and will judge all shooting by what they see.

The second consideration is that all pigeon shooting in this country is under statutory general licences (see Appendix 1) and one of their conditions is that birds 'must be killed in a quick and humane manner'. The licences recognise that some wounding of birds inadvertently occurs but require all reasonable effort be made to minimise it.

The BASC's ballistics and shooting research aims to provide the basis for practical guidance – best practice – on gun/cartridge combinations, together with shooting skills, to achieve consistently high kill levels on each quarry type.

We rely greatly on thirty-plus years of detailed, science-based fieldwork in the USA, under Tom Roster, of the North American Cooperative Shotgunning Education Programme (CONSEP). We simply cannot reproduce this work in this country, but believe it is sound and the best-available guidance on how to achieve consistently high success rates in sporting shooting.

Roster's work focuses on shooting skill – the ability to hit the target accurately and consistently

– and the essential combination of pattern density and pellet size. It starts with the principle that damage to vital organs (heart, lungs, brain, etc.) is what kills quickly. Pellet strikes elsewhere may well kill the bird eventually but it may suffer and never be retrieved.

Whether enough pellets fatally damage vital organs depends on pattern density and their penetrative energy. That energy crucially depends on pellet size - the larger the pellet the more potential energy it has to punch through feather, skin and muscle to reach the well-protected vital organs.

So, how does this work in practice? Roster has done so much already for us, through recording the outcome of each shot from thousands of hunters, guns, chokes, shot loads, pellet sizes and shot materials, over many ranges and quarry types. He finds that, provided a gun/cartridge combination produces a minimum pattern density at the maximum range at which a hunter can consistently hit the target, and that the pellet is the right size, then at least 90% of birds shot will be killed. All the hunter has to do is pattern gun/cartridge choice and then place the pattern accurately on the target. Easy!

Here, then, is how to pattern your gun for pigeon shooting.

- The chosen cartridge is patterned by firing at least five cartridges - preferably more - from the same box against a suitable surface *at the range at which you can consistently hit pigeons (be honest!)*;
- the traditional 30-inch circle is placed over the centre of each pattern and pellet strikes counted;
- the five or more counts are averaged.

If the average is at least 140 then, potentially, that gun/choke/cartridge combination should achieve high lethality on pigeons - provided they are not shot at a range when the pattern count falls below 140(ish), and the pattern is centred on the birds. In this context, the bore of shotgun used is irrelevant, provided it produces this pattern density from suitable cartridges.

What do we know about pattern densities and ranges at which pigeons are shot? Some years ago the BASC asked many pigeon shooters to estimate the range at which pigeon decoys were set out, both near the ground and in the sky, and to say whether they would shoot at birds at the test ranges. We also asked what their preferred pigeon cartridges were.

Most shooters underestimated the true range, especially at the longer distances, and often badly - for, example, more than half thought a sixty-yard bird was only forty yards away. Next, while nearly everybody said they would shoot the twenty-five and thirty-five yard birds, some three-quarters of shooters said they would shoot the pigeons that were fifty and sixty yards away. Finally, their favourite cartridge was 32g, then 28g and 30g, of No.6.

We patterned a widely-used 32g No.6 cartridge over thirty to sixty yards. At thirty yards any choke delivered well over the 140 'Roster' minimum (around 230 pellets). At forty yards only half-choke or tighter delivered the minimum count. At fifty yards the count was around 100 and at sixty yards it was 65. Clearly, a 30g or 28g load, as more recently found to be the favourite weight, would be even more limited by range as it contains fewer pellets to start with.

Although this trial focused only on pattern density, it had to conclude that woodpigeons were unlikely to be killed consistently by the favourite 32g No.6 much beyond forty yards. Bear in mind the previous finding of frequent underestimation of range - those results suggest many pigeon shooters would actually have been using this cartridge well beyond forty yards. How many can consistently centre their patterns on birds at even forty yards?

What about pellet size? We fired the same 32g No.6 loads at some recently-killed pigeons at thirty and fifty yards and then X-rayed the bodies. At thirty yards, typically, many pellets hit and then penetrated deeply into the body. At fifty yards, pellet strikes were few, often pellets lodged just under the skin, rarely penetrating deeply towards vital organs. Kill rates at thirty yards appeared potentially high but at fifty yards many hit birds would have been 'crippled' only, with most of those probably lost and wasted.

WOODPIGEON SHOOTING – HOW DOES SCIENCE HELP US DO IT BETTER?

More recent studies are revealing more about the effect of range, shooter skill and pellet size on successful pigeon shooting. We use Roster's classification of B1 = bird dead within 30sec, B2 = bird not dead or immobile within 30sec but retrieved and dispatched, B3 = bird hit but not retrieved, B4 = missed!

When shooters of varying abilities used the old favourite 32g No.6 we found that the number of B1s (dead) fell by half when range increased from twenty yards to fifty. The B3s (lost) doubled over the same increase of range. Combining B1s and B2s – i.e. all shot birds that were retrieved, whether dead or not – the most experienced shots achieved at least 80% kill-and-retrieve rates between thirty and forty yards, but not between forty and fifty yards. However, the novice shots could not kill 80%, even between twenty and thirty yards. These findings show the importance of a good dog to retrieve shot birds.

Ongoing research is now focused on lead loads of 28g No.7½; 30g No.5 and No.6 and a steel load of 32g No.4. Each load has been patterned over thirty to fifty yards. All produced the 140 minimum pellet count at thirty yards and forty yards but the pattern density fell away rapidly thereafter and none of the loads produced it at fifty yards. The next stage is field shooting trials on pigeons using a cross-section of shooting skill levels to help identify the strengths and weaknesses of each of these loads for successful pigeon shooting.

The main determinant of success, however, is the shooter's own skill. We can chop and change, test and re-test cartridge after cartridge to find which works best, but if we cannot place the pattern accurately and consistently on the target our shooting – and the pigeon – will suffer. We all like to think we can shoot if not well, then at least quite well. But what does that mean? Again Roster has been there before us and measured the shooting skill level of thousands of American hunters.

On a basic crossing clay, two-thirds of shooters have difficulty in hitting targets at twenty yards and three-quarters the same at thirty yards. To date, under 0.1% of American hunters have been able to hit six out of eight crossing clays at forty yards! The common response here is 'Ah, but that's the Americans …' but, perhaps uncomfortably, the BASC's (much smaller-scale trials) have shown similar results in this country too.

So, what does the science to date tell us? First, it helps us understand what it takes to kill a pigeon quickly and humanely. It is clear also, that even if every pigeon shooter used the gun/cartridge combination that all the research showed was the most effective at killing pigeons stone dead, their shooting success would vary considerably.

Individual shooting skill and self-discipline are the main factors determining shooting success. If we cannot consistently hit our pigeons at thirty, or forty, or fifty yards, then we should not shoot at those ranges. We can improve our shooting skills by ensuring good gun fit and gun mounting, and through practising with coaches and on clay targets.

If our chosen cartridge does not produce a killing pattern (measured here as at least 140 pellets in the 30-inch circle) at our personal maximum shooting range, then we should find a cartridge that does (by more patterning) and/or shoot closer with it. On pellet size, the jury is currently out and more research is needed.

What may well be true is that a very good shot, who can consistently centre his (or her) pattern on both the incoming and the high crossing pigeon, is likely to be successful with almost any sensible gun/cartridge combination. Most of us, however, are going to need more help to do well, and there is some useful science available to give us some practical help.

John Harradine
5 December 2011

ASSOCIATIONS

British Association of Shooting and Conservation (BASC)
Marford Mill, Rossett, Wrexham LL12 0HL
Tel: 01244 573000
www.basc.org.uk

Country & Land Business Association
16 Belgrave Square, London SW1X 8PQ
Tel: 020 7235 0511
www.cla.org.uk

The Countryside Alliance
The Old Town Hall, 367 Kennington Rd., London SE11 4PT
Tel: 020 7840 9200
www.countryside-alliance.org.uk

Game & Wildlife Conservation Trust
Fordingbridge, Hampshire SP6 1EF
www.gwct.org.uk

National Gamekeepers' Organisation
PO Box 246, Darlington DL1 9FZ
Tel: 01833 660869
www.nationalgamekeepers.org.uk

National Organisation of Beaters and Pickers Up
PO Box 292, Framlingham, Suffolk IP13 9FA
Tel: 08456 345014
www.nobs.org.uk

Royal Society for the Protection of Birds (RSPB)
The Lodge, Sandy, Beds SG19 2DL
Tel: 01767 680551 (office hours)
www.rspb.org.uk

FURTHER READING

Books
Arnold, Richard, *Pigeon Shooting*, Faber & Faber, 1961
Baker, Max, *Sport with Woodpigeons*, Shooting Times, 1934
Batley, John, *The Pigeon Shooter*, Swan Hill Press, 1995
Brander, Michael, *Sporting Pigeon Shooting*, A and C Black Ltd., 1986
Coats, Archie, *Pigeon Shooting*, André Deutsch, 1963
Coles, Charles, *Shooting Pigeons*, Percival Marshall & Co., 1964
Gray, John, *Pigeon Shooting*, The Crowood Press, 1988
Hall, Peter, *Practical Pigeon Shooting*, The Crowood Press, 1995
Humphreys, John, *Shooting Pigeons*, David and Charles, 1988
Johnson, A.E.B., *Shooting Wood-pigeon*, Herbert Jenkins Ltd, 1961
Murton, R.K., *The Wood-pigeon*, Collins New Naturalist, 1965
Theobald, Peter and Smith, Paul, *The Woodpigeon the Ultimate Quarry*, Ultimate Press, 1996
Verdet, Pierre, *La Palombe et Ses Chasses*, Edition Deucalion et J. et D. Editions, 1991
Walsingham, Lord, *Field and Covert*, Badminton Library, Longmans Green, 1889
White, Gilbert, *The Natural History of Selborne*, J.M. Dent, 1976
Willock, Colin, *The Book of the Wood Pigeon*, White Lion Books, 1995

Reports
Colquhoun, M.K., *The Wood Pigeon in Britain*, HMSO, 1951
Cramp, Stanley, *Territorial and other Behaviour of the Wood Pigeon*, Bird Study, 1958
Harradine, John and Nicola Reynolds, *Woodpigeons, Woodpigeon Shooting and Agriculture*, Report to BASC Council, 1993
Inglis, Ian and A.J. Isaacson, *The Responses of Wood Pigeon to Pigeon Decoys in Various Postures*, MAFF, 1983
Inglis, Isaacson and R.J.P. Thearle, *Longterm Changes in the Breeding Biology of the Wood Pigeon in Eastern England*, MAFF, 1994
Murton, R.K., N.J. Westwood and A.J. Isaacson, *A Study of Wood-pigeon Shooting, The Exploitation of a Natural Animal Population*, MAFF, 1974

WILL GARFIT PIGEON SHOOTING PRINTS

Illustrations from this book are published as 10 Limited Edition prints from Will Garfit's original paintings each is signed by the artist and available unframed.

All prints are 11 in x 8 in and full colour.

1. Coo-cooo-coo, coo-coo

2. Pigeons over the Decoys

3. Display Flight

4. The Nest

WILL GARFIT PIGEON SHOOTING PRINTS

5. Pigeon Country

6. Pigeon Pie

7. The Lost Bird Retrieved

8. Farmer's Lament, Pigeon Shooter's Joy!

9. Archie Coats in Action

10. Roost Shooting

1. Coo-coo-coo, coo-coo
2. Pigeons over the Decoys
3. Display Flight
4. The Nest
5. Pigeon Country
6. Pigeon Pie
7. The Lost Bird Retrieved
8. Farmer's Lament, Pigeon Shooter's Joy!
9. Archie Coats in Action
10. Roost Shooting

Prints available unframed at £25.00 each or £200.00 per set of ten inc. vat and p & p.
online: www.williamgarfit.co.uk
or cheque with order:

to
William Garfit, R.B.A.
The Old Rectory
Harlton
Cambridge CB23 1ES

INDEX

Acorns 81
Agriculture 80
Arnold, Richard 20, 187

Baker, Max 20, 187
Barley 69, 76
BASC (British Association of Shooting and Conservation) 13, 63, 186
 Woodpigeon Working Group 23
Batley, John 20, 187
Beans 69, 79
Beasley, Philip 52
Beech mast 81
Binoculars 43
Blue-rock 17
Bow saw 57
Brander, Michael 20, 187
Breeding Bird Survey (BBS) 24
Brolly 54 (*see also* Umbrella)
Brunt, Don 7
BTO (British Trust of Ornithology) 24, 33

Camouflage nets 44-5
Carrion crows 72
Cartridges 37
CLA (Country and Land Business Association) 186
Clay pigeon 90-1
Clothing 60

face mask 61
 gloves 61
 hat 61
 jacket 61
 overtrousers 61
 thermal underclothing 62
Coats, Archie 9, 11, 22, 41
 Pigeon Shooting 22, 40, 187
Coats, Prue 11, 41
Coles, Charles 20, 187
Collared dove, description 19
Collins Bird Guide 20
Colquhoun, M K 23, 187
Columba livia 18
Columba oenas 17
Columba palumbus 15
Counter (clicker) 55
Countryside Alliance 186
Cramp, Stanley 187

Decoying 64, 110-19
Decoys 47
 artificial 48-9
 cradles 51
 flapper 51
 floaters 50
 natural 47, 110
 patterns 110-13, 119
 peckers 54
 rotaries 52-3, 75, 114-5
Defra (Department of Environment, Food and Rural Affairs) 24

Digweed, George 77, 94, 160-1
Dogs 56-7, 76, 115-6, 124, 134
Double hide 93-4, 108

Ear muffs 55
Equipment 40, 42

Farmer
 farm guidelines 88
 permission 86
Faulds, Richard 94, 168-9
Feral pigeon 18
Flags 58-9
Flight lines 128-9
Folding saw 55

Game Conservancy 24
Game dealer 127
Garfit, Henry 154-6
Gas guns 66, 74
General licence 6, 18, 23, 181
Gina's recipes 140-6
Gloves 55
Gray, John 20, 187
Green, Chris 50
Guides 83
Gun 35
 .410 35
 12 bore 35
 20 bore 35
 28 bore 35
 chokes 36

190

INDEX

fitting 34
mounting 35
over and under 34-5
safety 34
semi-automatic 36
side by side 34-5
GWCT (Game and Wildlife Conservation Trust) 24, 186

Hall, Peter 20, 187
Hammer 58
Handguard 55
Harradine, Dr John 6, 181-2, 183-5, 187
Hetherington, Will 7
Hide poles 43
Hides 101-110
Hill, Andy 104, 151-4
Humphreys, John 20, 187

Inglis, Ian 187
Ivy berries 70

Johnson, A.E.B. 20, 187
Johnston, Andrew 14

La Palombière 32-3
Live pigeon shooting competition 38
Lofting poles 60, 133
Loppers 57

MAFF (Ministry of Agriculture, Fisheries and Food) 24, 25
Maize 68, 70
Ministry of Agriculture 23
Mobile phone 55
Murton, Dr R K 7, 20, 29
The Wood-pigeon 187

National Organisation of Beaters and Pickers Up 186
NFU (National Farmers' Union) 23
NGO (National Gamekeepers' Association) 186

Oilseed rape 22, 66-70, 72-3, 76-8,
Olstead, Jeffery 6, 13
Oxford Dictionary 20

Peas 71, 75, 79, 148-150
Puddifer, Martin 7

Quiller Press 14

Rabbit Clearance Societies 23
Racing pigeon 18
Recipes 140-6
Recoil pad 55
Reconnaissance 95-6
Rock pigeon 18
Roost shooting 63, 130-6
Rope bangers 55
Rotary decoys 52-3, 75
RSPB (Royal Society for the Protection of Birds) 24, 186
Rucksack 43

Sacks 58
Sainsbury-Plaice, Charles 7
Seat 46
Secateurs 55
Shooting
  footwork 35
  getting permission 86
  mounting 35
  opportunities 83-9
  practice 90-1
  snow conditions 53
  taking the shot 116-20, 133-4
  technique 90-2
  with friend 83, 93
Sound moderator 36
Spade 57
Stanbury, Percy 10
Stancliffe, Paul 33
Stock dove 17
Streptopelia decaocto 19
Streptopelia turtur 19
Stubbles 79, 179-81
Sunglasses 55

Theobald, Peter 20, 176-7, 187
Transistor radio 55
Travel bag 55
Turtle dove 19

Umbrella 42, 107, 108, 119, 157, 158, 174
Vehicle 41, 98-9, 101
Verdet, Pierre 187

WAGBI (Wildfowlers' Association of Great Britain and Ireland) 47
Walkie talkies 55
Walsingham, Lord 187
Waterproof coat 55
Waterproof trousers 55
Watts, Rupert 7
West London Shooting School 10
Wheat 78
White, Gilbert 187
Wildlife and Countryside Act 23
Willock, Colin 20
  The Book of the Wood Pigeon 187
Will's Shoot 14
Will's Shoot Revisited 14
Will's Shooting Ways 14
Windbreak 58
Woodpigeon
  breeding habits 26
  description 15
  history 21
  migration 31, 152
  monthly feeding pattern 63-82
  plucking, cleaning and breasting 137-9
  population 23
  predation 32
  recipes 137-6
  shooting clubs 85
  shooting equipment 40-62
  signed prints 188-9
  summer shooting 25
Wounded birds 120

Good teamwork at the end of the day.
(Rupert Watts)